TWAYNE'S WORLD AUTHORS SERIES

A Survey of the World's Literature

Sylvia E. Bowman, Indiana University
GENERAL EDITOR

NORWAY

Leif Sjöberg, State University of New York
at Stony Brook
EDITOR

Tarjei Vesaas

(TWAS 100)

TWAYNE'S WORLD AUTHORS SERIES (TWAS)

The purpose of TWAS is to survey the major writers —novelists, dramatists, historians, poets, philosophers, and critics—of the nations of the world. Among the national literatures covered are those of Australia, Canada, China, Eastern Europe, France, Germany, Greece, India, Italy, Japan, Latin America, New Zealand, Poland, Russia, Scandinavia, Spain, and the African nations, as well as Hebrew, Yiddish, and Latin Classical literatures. This survey is complemented by Twayne's United States Authors Series and English Authors Series.

The intent of each volume in these series is to present a critical-analytical study of the works of the writer; to include biographical and historical material that may be necessary for understanding, appreciation, and critical appraisal of the writer; and to present all material in clear, concise English—but not to vitiate the scholarly content of the work by doing so.

Tarjei Vesaas

By KENNETH G. CHAPMAN

University of California, Los Angeles

Twayne Publishers, Inc.   ::   New York

Preface

The greater part of the work on this book was done on two grants: the first a grant from the Research Committee of the University of California, Los Angeles, to do initial research on secondary literature in Norway during the summer of 1965, the second a Fulbright Research Grant to Norway during the academic year 1967–68, during which period the remainder of the necessary research was done and the book written. Thanks are extended to the members of the pertinent research committees and boards in general, and to the staff of the United States Educational Foundation in Norway in particular.

Thanks are also extended to the faculty and staff of the Institute for Scandinavian Language and Literature of the University of Oslo for making available reading-room facilities during both the summer of 1965 and the academic year 1967–68, and for their comments and suggestions at various stages of work on the book.

I would like to extend special thanks to Tarjei Vesaas for making available a set of proofs of his most recent book, so that a discussion of it could be included in this study, and for his cautious interest in my work.

Whenever possible, existing translations, either published or unpublished, have been used in quotations, as indicated in the footnotes. All other quotations have been translated by me expressly for use in this study. Changes have been made in the translations of others only when it has been necessary to do so in order to coordinate the language of the quotation and the discussion of it in the text.

K. G. C.

Contents

Chronology

1897   Born the oldest of three sons on the farm Vesaas in the parish of Vinje in Telemark, Norway.

1912   Finished grade school and was confirmed.

1917–
1918   Studied at Voss Folk High School.

1920   Began writing sketches, poems, and articles for local newspapers.

1921   Won first prize in a national magazine competition for a prose poem. A novel not accepted for publication.

1922   Won first prize in a short-story competition. A volume of prose poems not accepted for publication.

1923   The novel *Children of Man* published.

1924   Second novel, *Huskuld the Herald* published.

1925   First play, *The Pastor*, performed in Oslo. Also published a novel, *The Farm at Grinde*, and a play, *The Dwelling Places of God*.

1925–
1926   Traveled in Sweden, Denmark, France, Italy on government fellowship

1926   *Evening at Grinde, or The Good Angel*, a novel.

1927–
1929   Second journey abroad (18 months). Lived mostly in Munich. Visited Belgium, England, France.

1928   *The Black Horses*, a novel.

1929   *The Bell in the Knoll*, short stories.

1930   Bought the farm Midtbö in Vinje from his uncle, Oystein Vesaas. Published Part I of the Dyregodt tetralogy, *Father's Journey*. Still lived at Vesaas when in Norway.

1931   *Sigrid Stallbrokk*, Part II of the Dyregodt tetralogy.

1932   *The Unknown Men*, Part III of the Dyregodt tetralogy.

1932–
1933   Traveled in Czechoslovakia, Germany, Switzerland, France, Italy, Austria, Denmark.

1933   *The Sandalwood Tree*, a novel.

1934   Married the poetess Halldis Moren. Settled at Midtbö. Published Part I of the Bufast series, *The Great Cycle*, and a play, *Ultimatum*.

1935	Son Olav born. Published Part II of the Bufast series, *The Women Call: Come Home.*
1936	*The Clay and the Wheel,* short stories.
1938	*The Heart Hears Its Native Music,* Part IV of the Dyregodt tetralogy.
1939	Daughter Guri born.
1940– 1945	German ocupation of Norway.
1940	*The Seed,* a novel.
1945	*The House in Darkness,* a novel.
1946	Published first collection of poems, *The Springs,* and a novel, *The Bleaching Yard.*
1947	Published second collection of poems, *The Game and the Lightning,* and a play, *Morning Wind.*
1948	*The Tower,* a novel.
1949	*The Happiness of Travelers,* poems.
1950	*The Signal,* a novel.
1952	*The Winds,* short stories. (Awarded the Venice Prize in 1953.)
1953	*The Land of Hidden Fires,* poems.
1954	*Spring Night,* a novel.
1956	*May Our Dream Stay New,* poems.
1957	*The Birds,* a novel.
1959	*One Fine Day,* short stories.
1961	*The Fire,* a novel.
1963	*The Ice Palace,* a novel. (Awarded the Nordic Council Literary Prize.)
1964	*Collected Short Stories.*
1966	*The Bridges* a novel.
1968	*The Boat of Evening.*

CHAPTER 1

Intuition and Imagery in the Writings of Tarjei Vesaas

IN THE NEARLY fifty years that have passed since the publication of Tarjei Vesaas' first poems and stories he has produced a great number of works in a variety of forms and styles:
twenty-three novels, four volumes of short stories, and five volumes of poems, in addition to many separately published poems,
short stories and essays, and several stage plays and radio plays.
The topics he has taken up for treatment are similarly many
and varied. This extensive production is welded into a coherent
whole, however, by certain attitudes toward life expressed in it.
Before undertaking a chronological survey of his writings it will
be useful to discuss some of the most fundamental of these attitudes and their manner of expression, and this can best be done
by going directly to his books.

1 The Intuitive Apprehension of Reality

In the short story "Last Man Home" in the collection *The
Winds* (1952) an adolescent boy has a remarkable experience
out in the woods one day. He is hauling logs, as he has done
many times before. But he feels that there is something special
about the woods that day, without being able to figure out what
it is:

The hours pass. Smoke rises up among the spruce trees off at a distance. It is dinner time. The smell of smoke. The smell of frying. The
lumberjacks sit eating. Their hands are covered with resin. They have
been felling trees. Thousands and thousands of trees have risen up out
of the earth on these slopes.
This is where you belong, Knut.
What?—
No one said this, but this is what is happening today....
The woods open up before him. His life is revealed to him.[1]

11

When the work day is over he lets the others go on ahead home:

He stands there looking. Let the others go. Last man home.
Knut—
No one speaks his name. But still it seems to him that it is spoken. There it is again: Knut—. . .
Suddenly this evening becomes like an introduction, a consecration to an entire life among trees and taciturn men. He has never felt it so strongly before. . . .
This evening he experiences things as they really are: a great kinship. He has himself grown up out of slopes and valleys and hidden, seeping water. He is himself a fruit of this landscape. A child.
This evening his senses are open like a bowl.[2]

Such experiences, in which a person's sensitivity to his environment is intensified, so that he perceives well-known details in a new way and is able to grasp intuitively how they fit together in a coherent pattern, occupy a central position in Vesaas' writing. His characters frequently arrive at a certainty about their immediate situation or even the entire course of their lives in this way. In most instances Vesaas provides a realistic background for these experiences, describing vividly the sights, odors, or sounds on which they are based, as in "Last Man Home." Frequently, however, the reader is provided with few fixed points in reality for the understanding of such an experience, and it takes on a mystical, visionary quality. Such is the case in an earlier short story, called simply "The Vision" in the collection *The Clay and the Wheel* (1936). It begins:

They were talking about being sick and getting well, and things like that. That is, Hege and Jon were. Hege had a brother who was even smaller than she was. His name was Hallvar, and he was sick and wouldn't get well again for a long time.
"What Hallvar probaby needs is iron water," Jon said.
Hege innocently asked what iron water was.
Jon told her that it was what ran in red brooks. If it was calm a blue film formed on it. The sod along the edge of such brooks is red, and the stones at the bottom of them are red.
"Just like at Red Brook Marsh," Jon said and tried to be casual about it.
Hege wasn't fooled.
"You haven't known that very long," she said.
Jon was flabbergasted at her great wisdom, and confessed that he

learned about it only the day before. He had gone into the woods with his father and had *almost* been at Red Brook Marsh.[3]

Jon and Hege decided to go to Red Brook Marsh and get some iron water for Hallvar. They are a bit frightened by the forest and its inhabitants, but set off anyway. They come to the marsh and fill their little pails with water, but discover that it is no longer red when it is in the pails. They decide to take some home to Hallvar anyway, but when they try to find their way home they discover that the path has disappeared. To make matters worse, it is beginning to grow dark. They lose all hope, and sit down at the edge of the brook. Then suddenly something happens to Hege:

Just at that moment the thought of Hallvar came to her mind so distinctly that she bent over Jon and told him:
"I know something! Hallvar will soon be as well as we are."
"What?" asked Jon, who hadn't sensed what she had.
She was about to tell about it, but stopped, helpless, and felt ashamed. It was gone. She started stammering.
"Quick now!" Jon said curtly and gruffly. He was so close to her that his face loomed large.
"Hallvar will soon be as well as we are!" she said in confusion. "It seemed to me that Hallvar—that Hallvar—"
She looked down in shame. What she had said was gone. Jon hadn't been able to grasp it. She fumbled for it—Yes, he had grasped it! He was staring wildly at her.
And then they saw something: they were sitting in the middle of the path.
Right in the middle of the path. They stood up laughing. What's this? The path has come back! It wasn't darker than that they could see it easily. It was a crooked dark line through the forest, leading home with infinite certainty.
They couldn't understand how it could be, just understood that something good had happened and accepted it without question. They started walking away from Red Brook Marsh among the dim mounds. It didn't seem to them worth talking about how the path had risen up again from the depths—they just walked quickly off.
After a while they saw that their pails were empty. Hege said:
"It doesn't make any difference. He'll soon be as well as we are."
That reminded them, and they walked quietly on. Quietly and quickly. The path was so clear that they could have walked it asleep, but they weren't asleep now.
They merely cut through everything that met them at home: people

running and searching, stern questions, joy at their having shown up—merely cut through it. Get to Hallvar. He was asleep. But they had to see him. They knew something about him now. They were illuminated from within by a miracle.[4]

The sudden, clairvoyant experience, or vision, as Vesaas calls it, which Hege has is not based on the apprehension of any reality described in the story, but we can probably assume that it is based on her intuitive appraisal of her little brother's condition. As a result, both it and the rediscovery of the path by her and Jon take on a miraculous quality. The miraculous nature of their experience is underlined by the effect that it has on them: they are described as being "illuminated from within by a miracle." It should be noted, however, that this is a very everyday sort of miracle, performable by anyone, although in our modern, rational society the performance of such miracles is usually left to children.

There are, however, people who succeed in preserving into adult life the ability to apprehend and respond to reality in this direct, intuitive manner, and Tarjei Vesaas seems to be one of them, if we are to judge from the many descriptions of such experiences and the many sympathetic and uncannily perceptive portraits of children to be found in his writing. To suggest that Vesaas perceives the world as a child does is by no means disparaging; it is the necessary condition for all true poetic expression, if what the Swedish writer Stig Dagerman, who had a deep admiration for Vesaas' writing, has said is true:

> One starts being a poet early. All children are poets. But most people are weaned later on. So the art of being a poet consists, among other things, of not letting life or people or money break one of the habit.[5]

Vesaas has, to a higher degree than most people, perhaps even than most writers, preserved the native poetic ability displayed by children. This expresses itself not only in his faith in the intuitive apprehension of reality, but also in the prominent role he assigns to the evocation of visual images in his writing.

II   *The Evocation of Images*

The ability to transform what has been heard, or read or imagined, into visual images is described frequently by Vesaas, most often in connection with the experiences of children. For example, in the short story "The Cat," also in the collection *The Clay and the Wheel,* the story's main character, a little boy named Kristian, is hiding with his kitten under the currant bushes in the garden. He is trying to save his pet from the clutches of the "cat doctor," who has come to the farm to geld the kitten. His older sister, Inger, has come into the garden and is calling to him to come out with the kitten:

> Kristian wasn't listening. Just the thought of the cat doctor had given him a shock. Horrible tales appeared before him. He had heard them once, and now they had returned. Horrible images had formed in connection with the tales, and these images now spread themselves before his eyes. It was easy to form images. In connection with the kind of horrible tales *he* knew, they formed so lightning-quick that he almost fainted.[6]

The way in which such images can be perceived so intensely and vividly that they are experienced as reality, and the process of autosuggestion by which this can be accomplished, is well described in the novel *Spring Night* (1954). The main character in this novel is a fourteen-year-old boy who experiences daydreams and fantasies very intensely. One of his most common fantasies involves imagining that a snake is watching him when he is in his favorite spot out in the woods:

> I wonder if the snake is watching me? he thought.
> His skin prickled at the thought. I think it's watching me from a tiny hole. Just watching.
> A while later he said to himself:
> It must be watching me.
> Immediately he was positive:
> It *is* watching me—...
> No sooner had the image taken form than the pulling began.
> I'd better go home!
> He didn't mean it, he didn't want to go home, he wanted to feel that pulling, he wanted more and more to feel the strange spell that he thought had been cast on him from a hidden spot somewhere under a leaf.[7]

The boy feels the attraction of the snake in his fantasy as strongly as if there really were a snake present. Even after the spell has been broken the image which has formed in his mind continues to affect his perception of reality:

Was there something moving in the grass? He longed for there to be. A couple of blades of grass quivered and then were still again, or so it seemed to him.[8]

It should be noted that this is essentially the same type of experience Knut in "Last Man Home" has:

No one speaks his name. But still it seems to him that it is spoken. There it is again: Knut—

Although his name is in reality not being spoken, he reacts to the experience as if it were.

These two interrelated and somewhat mystical aspects of life: the intuitive apprehension of reality and the experiencing of a mental image as if it were reality, play important roles in Tarjei Vesaas' writing. In many of his stories and novels Vesaas does not tell a story in the traditional sense of the word, but presents, for the reader's intuitive acceptance, an image, or series of images, which expresses his impression of a life situation. This is true even in most of his works which, at least on the surface, appear to be "realistic." Behind the "real" story, however, there is also a series of impressions being communicated to the reader, the progression and development of which parallel the course of the "real" story. In this way there is achieved an interaction between the story and the images. The reader's apprehension of the images helps him understand the development of the story, and the progression of the story in turn helps him grasp the significance of the images.

Usually the connection between these two levels of image and story is clear, but frequently, especially in his more recent writing, Vesaas breaks this connection. This he does either by providing the images with no parallel story whatsoever, or with a story that makes no sense in realistic terms. The reader is forced to make associations without the help of any "real" story to serve him as a guide. This is a technique which is, of course, very common in contemporary poetry, and Vesaas employs it extensively in his poems, but he also makes frequent use of it in his prose writing. A good example of this is the story "Three Quiet Men" in his most recent collection, *One Fine Day* (1959). The choice of this story to illustrate this point is not casual. Its publication in 1959 signaled a major change in emphasis in Vesaas' writing, and it is in addition an excellent vehicle for the discussion of his use of images, both in his most recent and in his earlier writing. A translation of the complete text of the story follows.

THREE QUIET MEN

It was just by chance that it happened to be us three. Now, afterwards, we have become as one, but before that fatal day we knew each other only well enough for an occasional greeting.

We happened to meet one summer day on the way to the same river, with an afternoon of casual fishing as our common purpose. It was a warm day; our shirts clung to our backs. The path to the river swung past a low ridge thickly strewn with large, sun-baked boulders.

Our minds were on the simplest things; we talked about wind and weather and fishing luck—as men do when not forced to show other sides of themselves.

After a while we could hear the river rippling enticingly in the heat. One of us said:

"There's a path over the ridge here. There are marks on the stones. Why don't we take it?"

We did. The rippling of the river was so tempting that we took the harder but shorter way. We followed at the heels of him who had made the suggestion; he was wearing half-length rubber boots. We all wore rubber boots, and the tops of them slapped sharply against our legs as we leaped from stone to stone across the gaps between.

We never looked down at what was in the gaps, we caught only faint glimpses of dark openings as we jumped. They didn't concern us.

We had no trouble crossing the ridge, and there were now only a few last scattered boulders separating us from the promising river—

. . . without the slightest warning *The Shriek* broke out at our feet. We were suddenly surrounded by it. *The Shriek* flared up between two leaning stones, it resembled a skinned toad lunging and twisting and screaming before the jaws of a snake striped with yellow.

My God!—terrified by the sound, one of us quickly crushed the head of the snake with the heel of his boot. The snake had apparently done no harm: it was still full of venom, which ran like some sort of bitter sweat out of the crushed skull and down into the ground. The dry, sandy soil sucked it up. The rest of the snake danced about in constantly changing figure-eights, and would continue to do so until sundown, according to the old legend.

But there was no more time to waste on the snake. We had other things to think about. We stepped forward and grasped *The Shriek* with numbed hands. We had to—as though our lives depended on it. We had no idea which one of us did it; we were no longer three men with three pairs of hands—we were now *one*, and we grasped the inexpressible to hide it away.

Not a word. Just run.

We ran and ran with it. Got around the ridge probably as fast as anyone has ever made it. Ran on until we reached the nearest house, which was mine, and slipped in, half exhausted. Suddenly my house became the house for all of us—it was here that we had to hide this horrible thing.

There was no question of *why* we had to hide it—we *had* to, our lives depended on it.

But the sound did not cease once inside the house, and as we ran about, made senseless by *The Shriek*, we saw good neighbors running up with buckets in their hands to put the fire out. That is how it appeared to them. But they fled in equal haste and terror as soon as they had seen us. And we, we could only feel that we must not pause; we ran around the house and closed all doors and windows, stuck paper in keyholes and choked off all sound that would escape. We did this with motions not our own and panting for breath and without really knowing what we did.

That only made it worse. *The Shriek* lay there and sent up red tongues of flame and all openings out to the world were tight and dark and became tighter and darker for every minute. One last time we had to act, and with rolling eyes we moved forward and did the only thing our disordered senses could find to do: we grasped *The Shriek* and swallowed each our part of it and silence settled around us.

❊   ❊   ❊

Now we walk as if bearing lighted candles. We are three quiet men who can never part. We smile gently to all we meet, and those we meet send back friendly smiles to us, and do not know it.

About the proper approach to such a piece of writing Vesaas has written:

The reader must approach the reading without prejudice, so that he may be able to feel what the author is trying to get at. An author shouldn't write so that it can be understood with a cold heart. There should be a good deal that the reader can only *feel* inside himself. The reader must be allowed to open his own secret rooms. He must take part in the experience—and he can much more than he imagines at first, thank goodness.[9]

These words were written in connection with the difficulties many readers have had with the novel *The Fire* (1961), which was Vesaas' first novel after he wrote "Three Quiet Men," but

they apply equally well to this short story. In both these works
Vesaas uses precisely the same literary techniques, in one case
concentrated in a story of only several hundred words, in the
other case extended into the full novel form. The difficulties en-
countered in arriving at any meaningful interpretation of "Three
Quiet Men" arise primarily from the description of the nature of
"The Shriek." Its name would seem to indicate that it is a sound,
but it "flares up," as if it were fire. It is also described as resem-
bling a skinned toad which is at the mercy of a snake. It is, of
course, impossible to resolve the contradictions implicit in this
description within any realistic interpretation of the story. It
should not be difficult, however, for the reader to respond to it
as an image of something extremely terrifying and horrible, and
thus seen it is unimportant what its exact nature is. What is
important in the story is the reaction of the three men to it.

The first thing to notice about the three men's reaction to
"The Shriek" is that they transform it from an abstract image to
something which they experience as real and palpable. At first
the impression of "The Shriek" as fire is weak, and it is described
only indirectly, as flaring up. It ultimately becomes so real to
the three men, however, that they can see its tongues of flames,
and even grasp it. The similarity between the process being described here and the way in which the image of the snake becomes reality to the young boy in *Spring Night* should be clear.

It is important to notice that at the beginning of the story
the three men feel that the dark openings across which they are
jumping do not concern them, but that the appearance of "The
Shriek" in one of these openings makes it impossible for them
to maintain this attitude. They feel compelled to act, and do so
by grasping "The Shriek," however this might be possible in light
of its nature. This very act has an effect on the men: they cease
to be three, and become one. This is only a first step, however,
and leads to a greater crisis, indicated by the repetition of the
image of fire and by their increasing state of terror and confusion.
They once more act, this time by swallowing whatever it is that
they have been confronted by and which they no longer can
be unconcerned about. This final act transforms them completely.
They became illuminated, almost as if they have somehow become sanctified, and their very presence affects the lives of
others in a positive, if somewhat mystical, manner: "those we

meet send back friendly smiles to us, and do not know it." Their
transformation thus seems to be ethical in nature. They have gone
from a state of lack of concern and separateness to one of involvement and community as a result of having taken a standpoint to something extremely horrible and terrifying by nature.

Such an interpretation of "Three Quiet Men" is supported by
the appearance in it of images which have strong religious
connotations. The number 3 has religious or magical significance
in many cultures, and the associations wakened by the use of this
number are strengthened by the reference to lighted candles.
The image of light thus introduced is in turn contrasted by an
image of darkness, that of the openings between the rocks,
and it is not difficult in the context to see this light-darkness
contrast as representing a conflict between good and evil. These
implications are intensified by the appearance in one of these
openings of a snake, a common image of evil. The image of
darkness reappears just before the final act of the three men:
"all openings out to the world were tight and dark and became
tighter and darker for every minute," and it is their action to
prevent the impending total darkness from coming about that
leads to their illumination.

Such a broad interpretation of "Three Quiet Men" leaves
unanswered, of course, the question of the nature of the situation
which initiates the action of the three men and brings about
the change in them. Here the reader is left completely to his
own devices to arrive at any associations which the images used
arouse in him, based on his own personal experience. In this way
the story has much wider application than if Vesaas had chosen
to describe any one specific horrible or terrifying situation and
any one specific set of actions taken in response to it. What is
important in the story is that an act of commitment has taken
place, and this has had a positive effect on those involved.

III   The Recurrence of Images in Vesaas' Writing

A very important aspect of Vesaas' writing is the frequent
recurrence of images from one work to another. In this way all
of his writings are bound together and fit into a constantly
evolving and developing pattern. The recurring images become
motifs which run through his writing and give added signifi-

cance to it when seen as a whole. The use of an image in one work can also shed light on its significance in another work. This can be seen by looking at the way in which Vesaas uses some of the most important images in "Three Quiet Men" in other works.

The motif of three people joining together to perform an act leading to a good end appears in a perfectly realistic setting in the early novel *The Farm at Grinde* (1925). A little girl is lost, and a search party is out looking for her. She is found when one of the members of the search party happens to follow the flight of a hawk in his binoculars. The hawk circles over the girl, and she is seen, lying in a ravine far up on the mountainside. Three of the youngest and strongest members of the party volunteer to climb up and bring her down. The description of them is interesting when compared to that of the three quiet men:

The search party disbanded, each man headed home, and no one felt like talking.

The three vigorous men headed for the river. They stopped in at a house for a long rope, then hurried on. They crossed the bridge over the roaring, rushing river—and began climbing up.

No conversation between them, either.[10]

And after they have climbed up the mountainside:

And then they were up, and the ravine was directly below them. A little human being was lying down there, resting.

Silent men—they made their plans with few words, pointing, indicating to each other with facial expressions and gestures how they should proceed—silent silent men.[11]

Later, when they have returned the little girl safely to her mother, they are described as "three happy men." They bring happiness to the mother, and are happy themselves.

The same motif makes its appearance in the novel *The Bleaching Yard* (published 1946) in which the main character Johan Tander, is led to his moment of judgment and expiation by three men. In this case, the result of the action is tragic, but with strong positive overtones. In the structure of the novel there is nothing that necessitates there being three men involved in this action, and it would not have been in any way remarkable if there had been only two. Another example of the appearance of this motif will be found later in this chapter.

The feeling of shock and horror at the presence of a snake is one of the most important components of the impact which "Three Quiet Men" has on the reader. This is one of Vesaas' most frequently recurring motifs. A scene very similar in many ways to the central scene in "Three Quiet Men" is to be found in the story "Before Rain" in Vesaas' first collection of short stories, *The Bell in the Knoll* (1929). This story is a description of how a drought puts the small animals of the fields and woods at the mercy of a poisonous snake which has occupied the area around a spring, the only source of water left. A frog, made groggy by lack of water, crawls toward the spring despite the danger. The snake lets it come close, then lifts its head:

> Then the frog shrieks and comes to its senses. Struggles helplessly with its webbed feet, sees its deadly enemy leering at it snout to snout —how horrible to be in *his* power.[12]

Also in this case the snake is killed by a passing man before it can do the frog any harm, but here there is no significance for the man attached to the action: he merely walks on after having drunk from the spring. "Before Rain" is a story which vividly depicts the feelings of terror and horror which the presence of a snake can produce, but in this story the shriek of the frog is merely the outcry of a terrified creature, and no moral implications can be drawn from the action of the man in killing the snake, as can be done in "Three Quiet Men."

Fascination with evil, represented by fascination with snakes, is a motif which recurs frequently throughout Vesaas' writing. This is present only as an undercurrent in "Before Rain," whereas it is central in the scene in *Spring Night* quoted earlier, in which an adolescent boy effectively hypnotizes himself in this manner. Even more intense in its feeling of combined horror and fascination is the poem "The Path of the Snake across the Rock" in the collection *The Happiness of Travelers* (1949):

> The sun-warmed rock
> is smoothly, softly rounded,
> with hot, sloping sides
> —no one ventures there.

> No one has met anyone.
> Never were there tracks in the stone.
> Never the rustling of heather.
> The rock radiates horror.

> Like an icy gliding
> over a warm breast—
> but rock is mute,
> rock shouts nothing
> before that day comes
> when both rock and cloud will cry out.
>
> And the snake glides past,
> slowly polishing the rock
> on its errands,
> and the bird that is to perish
> sings.

There are any number of points of similarity between this poem and "Three Quiet Men." Not only the presence of the snake, but also the sun-warmed mass of stone (boulders in "Three Quiet Men") and the innocent living creature that is threatened, as well as the presence, or in the poem the potential, of a horrified or terrified outcry. It also resembles "Three Quiet Men" in that, although the images are all taken from the reality of nature, they express more than can be grasped by any strictly realistic interpretation of them. Rocks and clouds never "cry out" in any realistic sense of the word, and the reader is left feeling that something is implied by the use of this image that he must try to sense intuitively.

The contrast between light and darkness which plays such an important role in "Three Quiet Men" is one of the most important motifs in Vesaas' writing. Several of his novels reflect it even in their titles, e.g., *The Black Horses, The House in Darkness, The Bleaching Yard,* and *Spring Night* (note that spring nights in Norway are very light). In "Three Quiet Men" it is connected with the illumination of the three men as a result of their action when confronted by "The Shriek." They seem to those they meet to be bearing lighted candles. The concept of people as bearers of light is frequent in Vesaas' writing. It is found in a realistic setting in his early novel *Huskuld the Herald* (1924). Huskuld is an old man whose wanderings through the world make up the main part of the novel. At one time during his wanderings Huskuld meets a happy young boy and a happy girl whose sheer joy of living cheers him up:

They are bearers of light, beautiful candles, placed on this earth at long intervals. They shine, and make life livable for others. . . . And now Huskuld had one on each hand.

Huskuld, where are you now. He was like an old father who was leading his children out into the world, one on each hand. And the world smiled to them, and was still friendly toward them, and they were friendly to the world in return, and would stand there lighting up the darkness.[13]

Here, as in the final paragraph of "Three Quiet Men," the emphasis is on the positive effect the light-bearers have on those around them. In this case this aspect of their nature is described as "this gift from a good God which some people receive," whereas in the much more recent work "Three Quiet Men" it has, as we have seen, been attained by means of a much more complex psychological process involving facing up to some sort of horrible situation or fact of life and being transformed by this act of involvement.

This motive assumes a much more mystical quality in a passage toward the end of *Huskuld the Herald*. Huskuld is now ill and dying. A three-armed candelabra which has figured earlier in the novel as an instrument of defeating the "forces of darkness" has been burning in the room where he is lying. During a fever-ridden dream he has been having he imagines that he sees a light off at a distance.

And just then lamps began burning off at a distance, and when he came closer to them, they grouped themselves together in one spot and stood there in a shining row of three.

"My candelabra!" he said, and saw that he was home.[14]

But he dozes off again, and his next fever dream begins:

Sull lull into a land of blueness. Three men in an enchanted valley, what else?

Shuffle-shuffle, three men in the snow, walking in a row at each other's heels. Those behind stepped in the footprints of the one in front of them, they were walking through an enchanted valley, the light was fading and there was the sound of shuffling as they walked along. . . .

And the men walked along, and they were silent, that's true, and they didn't know where they had come from, if anyone had questioned them about it, nor did they know where they were headed, if the questioner had been curious about that.

No, far from it, they were only three shuffling men.[15]

But after they have walked through the darkening valley a while something happens:

> And after they had walked for a long time through the grayness and the quietness each of them noticed a little light above the other two. Just a glimmer, but still a light; they could see it clearly against the darkness of the enchanted valley and its light fell on the snow around. They were puzzled by this, and tried to extinguish the lights in every way they could, but they just kept burning calmly, and then they decided that the lights were something they had been given and which were to be theirs.[16]

As they walk through the valley they see empty wolf pits, then wolf pits containing dead people, then a group of still living people digging pits for themselves to lie in:

> The group never saw the three men coming, as if they had been invisible to them. But still, they must have felt something passing, because they paused in their work and stared and suddenly a new look came to their eyes, a distant longing for something better.[17]

This scene in the novel is connected with Huskuld's role as a herald of better things to come, but it should be easy to see how closely it is related to "Three Quiet Men" in its use of images. It is only one of several dreams and visions which Huskuld has in the course of the novel and which are always carefully provided with a realistic background. In this case, for example, the reader can assume that the sight of the three-armed candelabra served as the basis for Huskuld's dream fantasy, and this in turn can serve the reader as a basis for associations which will help him interpret the function of the dream within the structure of the novel. The failure of Vesaas in much of his more recent writing to provide the images he describes with a realistic background within the works themselves places great demands on the reader, but it also offers the possibility of great rewards. The successful reading of such a piece of writing must be a much more personal experience than is usually the case. The reader is required to apply his own experience of life to the images and situations described, and in this way must become more a participant in the artistic process than a spectator to it.

It should be clear that a considerable development in literary technique has taken place between the appearance of the motif of the contrast between light and darkness in these scenes in the early novel *Huskuld the Herald* and its appearance in "Three Quiet Men" thirty five years later. Much of the discussion of Vesaas' writing in the following chapters will center around this development.

CHAPTER 2

Vesaas' Earliest Writings —1920-1926

AT THE shining age of twenty just about everyone writes poems. It's such an easy thing to resort to then. It seems as if you have a blank page inside you, and that it's there for poems to be written on. And poems do appear on that page, as if from nowhere—out of joy, or longing and despair. And the temptation to write them down on paper can be too strong, and so they are written down and hidden away. Or *perhaps* allowed to appear in the light of day in a kindly local newspaper.[1]

These gently self-ironizing words tell much about the conditions under which Vesaas started writing, and also about his attitude toward his early writing. The local newspapers were indeed kindly toward him, but he very soon began publishing stories and poems in national magazines and newspapers in the larger cities. The general nature of his early writing is well, though perhaps a bit too harshly, described in his own judgment of his second published novel, *Huskuld the Herald* (*Sendemann Huskuld,* 1924): "so romantic that is unreadable."[2] This novel, and most of Vesaas' early writing, is most certainly romantic, at times even sentimental, but if one first accepts its romantic nature, there is a great deal of readable material to be found there.

I Romantic and Religious Influences

We do not have to search long to find the sources of this romantic approach. About a volume of prose poems which was rejected for publication (perhaps fortunately) in 1922, Vesaas has written that they were "short prose poems, such as the great Tagore in India wrote, with phrases like those used by my idol Knut Hamsun, and full of romanticism in the style of my other idol Selma Lagerlöf."[3] As it turned out, other more lasting and benevolent literary influences were at work on Vesaas during these years but some time had to pass before the

27

heavy overlay of romanticism was worn thin enough for them
to show through clearly and decisively. Tagore's influence on
the budding writer can be traced to the translations from English of several of Tagore's books made by his teacher at Voss
Folk High School, Lars Eskeland. Vesaas writes enthusiastically
both of Eskeland as a teacher and of the Tagore translations
on which he was working during Vesaas' year at Voss. He writes
just as enthusiastically about Selma Lagerlöf, especially of
Gösta Berlings Saga, one of the most unabashedly romantic
novels in Scandinavian literature. And at this stage in Vesaas'
development it was certainly Knut Hamsun's early neo-roman-
tic novels (especially *Pan* and *Victoria*) which had the greatest
influence on his style.

Despite the heavy dose of romanticism in both style and
content, however, Vesaas' early writing displays a highly original, though frequently unbridled, talent. Early reviewers were
almost unanimous in predicting a brilliant, if unusual, writing
career for him, even when they criticized him in the same
breath for the excessive and transparent influences evident in
his writing.

In addition to its heavy overlay of romanticism, Vesaas'
earliest writing is characterized by frequent, often rapturous
and even sentimental, expressions of religious belief reflecting
traditional Christian attitudes. Typical of these expressions are
such passages as these from *The Farm at Grinde (Grindegard,*
1925): "May God watch over each little home in the woods!"[4]
and "... and a voice prays to be granted sleep in the precious
name of Christ—"[5]; from *Huskuld the Herald:* "May God watch
over all the animals in the woods."[6] (and see also the passages
quoted from *Huskuld the Herald* in Chapter 1); from *Children
of Man (Menneskebonn,* 1923): "... gentle Jesus, who paid with
his blood for the life and health of all of us."[7] The title of the play
The Dwelling Places of God (Guds bustader, 1925) is a quotation
from Revelations 21, and the content is accordingly religious.

This tendency toward religious sentimentality in Vesaas' early
writing is closely connected with its overall romantic flavor,
and can undoubtedly be at least partially ascribed to the same
literary sources, but in addition there were probably some en-
vironmental influences at work on Vesaas from the strongly
pietistic attitudes common at the beginning of the twentieth

century in Norwegian rural communities, of which the township of Vinje is quite typical.[8] As in the case of the romantic influences, these influences from traditional religious attitudes were not lasting, and the excesses to which they led soon disappeared from his writing.

Closely related to the romantic and religious strains in Vesaas' early novels, plays, and poetry, is the highly unrealistic attitude toward women in these works. There is an ethereal, madonna-like glow to most of these early Vesaas women. Liv Myrejard in *Children of Man* is even referred to as "Madonna" by the two men who love her. Lis in *Evening at Grinde* (*Grindekveld*, 1926) is time and time again referred to as Toremun's "good angel" and the novel is subtitled *The Good Angel*. It is parenthetically interesting to note that she is also twice referred to as being his good fetch, tales of fetches being widespread in Norwegian folklore and having their origin in Scandinavian mythology, which only serves to add to the reader's confusion about the function of the religious beliefs expressed in these books. Only Tuve in *The Dwelling Places of God*, who bears the child of one brother while married to the other, shows any tendency to behave in a non-angelic fashion, but even her behavior and its consequences serve primarily as a vehicle for moralizing on the part of the author. In this respect, too, Vesaas showed rapid changes in attitude, and in his later books, although women are still looked upon as a primary source of all that is good (due to their close connection with the creative processes of birth and regeneration), his early uncritical, romantic portraits of women give way to more rounded, realistic ones.

II *Themes*

The basic themes of these earliest works are also derived from traditional Christian attitudes: the will to sacrifice oneself for others, and the will to do pennance. As examples of these attitudes we can take Liv Myrejard in *Children of Man*, and Toremun in *The Farm at Grinde* and *Evening at Grinde*.

Liv is loved by two men. One of them is Knut Heddejor, the novel's main character, whose mother died while giving birth to Knut. The circumstances under which he was born hung over him like a secret burden of guilt. That is how it felt for him

to have had his life paid for so dearly. And he sort of gathered everything beautiful he saw and heard, wove it all together into strange
dreams, and composed a memory of mother out of it, an image infinitely lovely and delicate.[9]

Knut meets Liv under dramatic circumstances: he is lost
in the mountains at night in the wintertime and would have
died if he had not come across the bloody tracks of another
man in the snow. He follows the tracks and comes to a house.
The other man, Liv's brother, is dying, and Liv's beautiful pale
face and large, sad eyes make a deep impression on him: "He
looked at that deathly pale face as at a vision."[10] Knut later tells
Liv how he imagines his mother to have been:

I think she must have been like you. It is as if she hadn't died. . . .
Perhaps her spirit has entered you, so that she could return to her
son."[11]

He tells Liv that he could not have survived the tribulations
of life if he had not met her. Liv is fond of Knut, but really
loves another man, Torstein, who also loves her. But Liv
(whose name means "life") feels she must sacrifice her love for
Knut's sake. Torstein is puzzled by her attitude toward him,
but when he discovers the reason for it, he is happy.

Thus, Liv's sacrifice makes not only Knut, but also Torstein,
happy. Later, after she has died in a blizzard, Knut and Torstein join company and go to Heddejor, where Knut was raised
by his grandfather. Knut, who is a blacksmith, and Torstein
then make a large wrought-iron cross and carry it on their
backs the many miles to Myrejard, to raise it in memory of Liv
—and thus find deliverance from all their sorrows and pain.

Toremun, the central character of the Grinde novels, throws
an innocent lamb (!) into the rushing outlet of a mountain
pond. He does this in a fit of depression and anxiety, though
imagining that he is doing it for the sake of Brit, a girl he has
grown up together with and with whom he is falling in love.
He is then overwhelmed by remorse and longs to make good his
misdeed. He goes into the mountains, looking for lost lambs
to save, longing to "take the lamb on his shoulder and carry
it and do penance."[12] He spends the summer in this way, and
"when he finally returned home to Grinde he had found con-
solation and help, had won out, even if the agony might someday come back."[13] And the "agony" does come back. In the final

section of *The Farm at Grinde,* Toremun accidently kills Brit during a trip across the mountains in a blizzard, and once more he is obsessed with the desire to do penance, although he is totally innocent of any misdeed: "Oh, to suffer suffer, that's what I must do from now on...."[14]

Evening at Grinde opens with Toremun in jail, doing penance for a crime he did not commit, and even after it has become quite clear to the authorities that he is innocent (from hearing his feverish babbling when he lies ill in the prison infirmary), he still refuses to admit his innocence and to leave. The infirmary nurse, Lis, also tries to persuade him of his innocence, but in vain. She is falling in love with him, and leaves her job when she sees it is impossible to convince him. The rest of the novel tells of Toremun's decision to leave the prison and return to Grinde, and of the struggle in his mind between remaining true to the memory of Brit and giving in to his awakening love for Lis, his "good angel," who has devoted her life to trying to win him back to life. The book ends melodramatically, with Toremun being killed when he protects Lis from injury by a blasting charge, without Toremun's conflict really becoming resolved. As in *Children of Man,* the central themes of the Grinde novels are sacrifice and penance, expressed in traditional Christian terms.

Another theme, related to these, is common in all the early Vesaas works: that of a better time to come. It is expressed concisely in a speech from the play *The Dwelling Places of God:*

> But from all such suffering comes longing—we long for and ask about a better time. This earth is sort of the home of longing; everything alive seems to be longing.
> And if we want to attain this better time, when the dwelling place of God is with each human being, we have to keep our eyes fastened on it during our travels.[15]

These earliest plays and novels cannot be said to have been successful, despite occasional well-written nature descriptions and a few passages here and there which reveal true poetic talent. The religious themes which they contain, and the characters in terms of which they are presented, are in general treated much too superficially to be either interesting or enlightening.

The characters are for the most part figures rather than living people, and the religious and romantic clichés which are frequently used to describe their situations frustrate any attempt on the part of the reader to understand them and their plight. What makes these books interesting, and is the reason for discussing them in such detail, is that their central themes, however unconvincingly presented here, serve as a background for an understanding of the resolution of modern ethical conflicts which Vesaas arrives at in his later works.

III Style

There are certain aspects of these early works, however, which are interesting in themselves, and which also shed light on the development of his later style. One of the most characteristic features of Vesaas' writing is his tendency to assign unexpected qualities to objects and things in the world. An example of this in his later writing is "The Shriek," which has the qualities of both living things and fire. But this represents the end stage of a long development which appears to have had its origin in somewhat romantic and anthropomorphic descriptions of nature, for which Vesaas' most immediate model was probably similar descriptions in the novels of the nineteenth-century Norwegian writer Björnstjerne Björnson. The first chapter of Björnson's novel *Arne* (1859) is the classic example of this style in Norwegian literature ("How about covering the mountain," said the juniper bush.) A reading of the first paragraph of Vesaas' first published novel, *Children of Man,* shows that he has made skillful use of his model:

Even if Kjellborg Ridge is no mountain, it is still bare and rugged. Clusters of heather and dwarf birch live their life there. A lonely life. Every once in a while a covey of ptarmigans come sweeping through the air. White and cold in the winter, colorful and warm in the summer. Their visit is short, they come and go, a sudden whirring, and that is all. The dwarf birch is left behind, follows the flight of the sailing birds until they are out of sight, has caught a glimpse of a way of life that is light and spacious, a more beautiful life, but one unthinkable for one who is anchored in a marsh with long roots. And the dwarf birch hunches down, spreads itself out, an occasional bush stretches out from the clump of turf it stands on and mirrors its twisted body in Kjellborg Pond.[16]

Besides the personification of inanimate objects evident in this passage, it is interesting also for the presence, in embryonic form, of another important feature of style characteristic of Vesaas' writing: short, elliptical sentences alternating with clusters of sentences strung together without a break.

The personification of inanimate objects can serve other purposes than that of mere description. Another passage in *Children of Man* illustrates this:

How still the woods can stand after a snowfall. Each tree and bush bears its white burden, yes, even the smallest bushes, the weakest branches, all have their share to bear, and they stand so still so still, as if they were afraid to lose the least bit of what has been assigned to them.[17]

This passage appears at the beginning of the chapter in which Knut and Torstein leave for Heddejor after the death of Liv in the blizzard. The description of the snow as a burden each branch must bear serves in its context to symbolize the burden Knut and Torstein must bear because of Liv's death, and which is further symbolized by the iron cross which they later bear on their backs. Vesaas' use of objects in nature as symbols in his early works is also illustrated by the image of the mountain in *Children of Man*. It occurs first when Knut has left Heddejor after saving the life of a girl whom he loved, but who loved another. He feels he must leave the village, and sets out:

And in back of it all was the mountain; it was lofty and white and cold, but its peak pierced the clouds, and disappeared.[18]

After Torstein has found out that Liv Myrejard wishes to remain faithful to Knut he leaves Myrejard, where he has been working as a hired hand, and moves to his old home, a little farm beneath the mountain peak. This chapter is entitled "Beneath the Peak," and opens:

It is the mountain peak that reaches above everything. It is the first thing the morning sun gilds, and the last thing colored by the red evening sun. It rears its proud head at the sky, and cleaves the northern lights when they flood the sky with a storm warning.[19]

When Torstein's resolution to keep his relationship to Liv pure falters, he seeks inspiration in the sight of the mountain peak:

But then it was as if the peak rose up before his eyes, lofty and sharply etched, purer than anything else.

And facing this proud spire he felt that he, a human being, did not want to be the lesser man. He cried out angrily at the peak:

"Never, never shall you see me give in!"[20]

The mountain peak is used in both these cases to represent the strict ethical demands that Knut and Torstein make on themselves once they have decided to sacrifice their own interests. The image returns in the final sentence of the book, as Knut and Torstein carry their cross across the last stretch of heath to Myrejard: "On the horizon a peak rose up, lofty and sharply etched."[21] Both Knut and Torstein *have* been able to live up to the ethical demands they have made on themselves. The use of the mountain peak in this way is a bit romantic within the context of the book as a whole, but it is effective. Harald Naess, thinking of how Vesaas has frequently titled later novels on the basis of their central image, has suggested that the novel could very well have been titled *The Peak*,[22] and he is certainly right in this. The mountain peak in *Children of Man* is not as successful a central image as those in Vesaas' later novels, but it is an early example of a technique that was to play an increasingly important role in his writing.

IV   Huskuld the Herald

In Vesaas' second novel, *Huskuld the Herald*, Huskuld stands in a close relationship to the birds living in the woods which surround his tiny farm. He has no company except the birds he keeps alive in the wintertime with the grain he grows on his tiny plot of land:

The sparrows and titmice loved him dearly. Those blessed little things! They could soar all they wished between heaven and earth, they needed neither to sow nor reap, that was taken care of by their good father: Huskuld of Faltinbu, that was his mission in life.[23]

As can be seen from this quotation, both the sentimental and religious strains in Vesaas' early writing are prominent in *Huskuld the Herald*. But there is also much more there; in many ways it is one of the best books he has written, and by far the best of his early works. Huskuld's lonely life is broken when a gypsy woman and her little son, Ingebjönn, come to Faltinbu, hungry and cold. He feeds them and lets them stay the night. In the night the mother runs away, leaving her child with Huskuld. They grow very fond of each other, and when the mother returns for her child in the spring, Huskuld is heartbroken. He sets out to find another child to care for, but it must be one which would have nothing to lose by coming to live with him. He meets many people and sees many children, but none who would not be better off as they are. Discouraged, he is about to return home, when he finds out where Ingebjönn is. But during his travels he has also met a couple who have lost their only son. He realizes Ingebjönn will be better off with them, and allows them to take him into their home. He returns home alone. Shortly after, an unexpected and premature frost comes. In order to protect the grain for his beloved birds he covers it with all his blankets and even the clothes off his body. He saves much of the grain, but becomes ill and dies.

This is the first of several novels by Vesaas centering around journeys. The travelers in these novels receive many impressions of life during their journeys, and the effect of these impressions on them often reveals itself in strange visions and dreams which they have. One of Huskuld's dream visions has already been discussed (the "three men in an enchanted valley") in Chapter 1. Soon after he has come home he wanders aimlessly through the forest after a rainstorm. He comes to a rocky knoll projecting above the forest, and climbs it:

And when he had climbed up, what was there about it? Had the whole world been rinsed by the lightning and rain, or why was it so remarkably clear?

Was it maybe because Huskuld was not the same? But it was as if he was standing on a veritable mount of clarity. The mountains that usually framed in the picture surrounding him—today they melted away and could be seen through, just lay there like a thin film so that everything behind them was laid bare. Everything became so marvelously clear as the scales fell from his eyes.[24]

What Huskuld sees is that there is a better time coming for the people of the earth, and that they must keep faith and look forward to it, passing the faith on from generation to generation.

That same night Huskuld dreams that all human troubles "are smoke and shall be no more." This seems to be another reference to Revelations 21, from which also the title of the play *The*

Dwelling Places of God is taken. At the very end of the novel one of Huskuld's neighbors, who has heard that he has found out something important about life during his travels, comes to him and pleads with him to tell him why life is so difficult. Huskuld repeats these words in his delirium:

"It is smoke," he said, "and shall be no more."
[The neighbor] threw himself across the bed, as if to prevent Huskuld from leaving him. To no avail: Huskuld was already infinitely lightened, and something was calling to him and he went on and came to a home that he knew from before. A woman came out of the door, and he recognized her, oh yes, she was fair and tall as was everything there, and she opened the door and invited him to enter.[25]

That the ending of this novel is reminiscent of the ending of Ibsen's *Peer Gynt* is not surprising. Ibsen's plays, and *Peer Gynt* in particular, have always occupied a special place in Vesaas' attention,[26] and this is only one of many places in Vesaas' writing where echoes of Ibsen's works can be detected. At this point in his career Vesaas was most influenced by the romantic aspects of Ibsen's writing, but Ibsen's influence was to appear at deeper levels in later Vesaas books.[27] Romantic as it is, *Huskuld the Herald* has one thing in its favor that lifts it above his other novels from the 1920's: the figure of Huskuld himself. As unrealistically as he and his environment are portrayed at times, he is completely believable as a human being, and the reader can hardly help but be charmed by his naïveté and sincerity.

V   *The Beginnings of Development*

Despite the overall weaknesses of these early works, and the basic similarity of their religious themes and romantic styles, some development can be seen in them. A good example of this is the development which starts to take place in descriptions dealing with the clearing of land. When this motif first appears in Vesaas' writing, it does so in a highly sentimental form. In his early prize-winning prose poem "To My Sun-Maiden" from 1921 he gives vent to a series of rapturous feelings while describing his vision of life with an imagined sweetheart:

I will clear a farm, I will dig in the earth—we have a pact with the earth, she is our mother, she blesses her sons. . . . Look at the field,—

look, it is ripe now, the grain is golden now! Oh, ripe field! Oh, golden grain![28]

In a prose poetic sketch entitled "Flowers of the Earth" published the following year, he talks about "the newly cleared farm which sent up its shoots when will and love met—that must be the flower among the flowers of the earth."[29] This short sketch reappears two years later in a slightly altered form in *Huskuld the Herald*,[30] but one which leaves the romantic attitude toward the clearing of land intact. In *The Farm at Grinde*, however, published the following year, a new and deeper perspective is added. Grinde is a deserted farm when Toremun's parents come to work it, and they must first clear a field. In the beginning everything is still idyllic:

He stood there bent down to the earth and dug and strained and the stones he removed grew into piles; he sweated, but he was so young and he could smile although his back ached and the sun burned and the stones were so heavy. . . .[31]

A child is born to the couple, and the struggle becomes more serious:

The field grew in size, and the piles of stones grew in size, they were large silent memorials, but they also left their mark on him who had built them.[32]

The child dies, however, and a change takes place within the father. Clearing land is no longer the game it was:

. . . and the husband began to clear land in a sort of delirium, he had to stifle what was trying to strike him down, strike back at something; it was as if the earth trembled a little in fear before him as he dug in it with steel and force.[33]

In *Evening at Grinde*, after Toremun, the couple's second child, returns to Grinde after finally leaving jail, he, too, begins clearing land as if obsessed:

The son just grabbed the shovel in desperation, began digging blindly, . . . a clearer of land had probably never looked with such an expression on his face out over the field: why couldn't it spring to life, the joy which is part of such work?[34]

We are also given a quasi-psychological explanation of Toremun's nature, tracing it back to his father's:

The son had inherited so heavy and confused a spirit, and fate had then attacked him, grabbed hold of him and thrown him to the ground and then gone its way without the least explanation.[35]

Toremun is the first of many characters in Vesaas' books who are at the mercy of forces over which they have no control, and against which they struggle, sometimes successfully, sometimes in vain. He shows this side of his nature first in the sequence in *The Farm at Grinde* in which he throws the lamb into the pond. This is one of the most remarkable and haunting scenes Vesaas has ever depicted, and it stands out sharply in the novel, breaking as it does into the sentimental story of the childhood of Toremun and Brit. How difficult life is for Toremun, how strong the forces pulling at him are, is well described:

And so he bowed his head and realized once more how different life is for different people.

One person could laugh while another was plagued by riddles: one could just let evening and night come and face it with a light heart—while another felt the night blossom like dark flowers, and felt how it pulled and sucked and made him weak, so he had to approach it and try to get to know it, as one is always attracted by that which is hidden.[36]

He has come out into the night because he felt that he was "somehow being called," by something that is "calling and asking if I dare."[37] And he is fully aware of what is facing him: "Tonight I will try to find out who I am."[38] The conflict within Toremun is never clearly defined nor successfully resolved; the desire to do penance for the lamb's and Brit's death is not deeply enough grounded psychologically and the ending of the story too melodramatic for this. But the anxieties and obsessions which plague him are central human problems, and even though Vesaas was not able to present them convincingly at this early stage of his career, it is clear that the romantic attitudes toward life which characterize his early writing were already beginning to undergo a transformation.

CHAPTER 3

Years of Experimentation and Development
1928-1938

BETWEEN the publication of *Evening at Grinde* in 1926 and the novel *The Heart Hears Its Native Music* in 1938 Vesaas' writing underwent a tremendous development. His first novel during this period, *The Black Horses* (*Dei svarte hestane*, 1928), only partially continued the break with romanticism foreshadowed in *Evening at Grinde*. It is written in a style which is almost free of sentimental outbursts, and the basic religious orientation of his earlier books is totally lacking, but at the same time it is a throwback to the romantic novels of rural life which were so prominent in Norwegian literature in the nineteenth century.

I The Black Horses

The Black Horses is the story of Ambros Förnes and his family. Ambros owns four fine black horses, and he and his four children—two grown children by his first marriage and two small children by his second—are completely preoccupied with them. To Ambros' young second wife, Lisle, who does not share the enthusiasm of the others for the horses, "it is as if they all had been possessed by black horses."[1] Lisle does not love Ambros, and married him only for her parents' sake, although she loved another man. When Ambros finds this out he takes to drinking and horse racing. He finally ruins himself, and loses his farm and his horses. Told with any degree of psychological insight, this story could engage the reader, but for the most part Vesaas substituted melodrama for psychological insight, and the resulting novel is of little interest as a whole. There are, however, some fortunate exceptions to this. This is particularly true of the portrayal of Ambros' and Lisle's six-year-old son, Kjell. He is the immediate forerunner of Jon and Hege in "The Vision" and Kristian in "The Cat," and the first of many brilliant portraits of

39

children in Vesaas' writing. Torn by his natural feelings of love
for both his parents, who use him as a pawn in the struggle between them, he withdraws into his own world of fantasy and
comes close to psychological catastrophe. After the death of his
father he flees from his mother, and is drawn back to her, and to
life, only by the overwhelming need for love which he feels. The
resolution of the struggle in which he is engaged with himself
comes one afternoon when he is out skiing by himself:

A couple of hours passed like this, and Kjell thinks about all sorts
of things. Then suddenly it is as if a mighty wave sweeps over him:
mother! Finally what has been lying there smoldering breaks out:
mother! He has to go to her. Nothing but this: he has to go to his
mother. He stands there trembling. A bird calls in the woods: he is so
lost in his thoughts that he thinks it is his mother calling. Yes, now he
hears it clearly. He dashes into the woods. Kjell! it calls.[2]

Unfortunately, the manner in which the certainty of his feelings for his mother comes to Kjell is vague. The reader is not presented with an image or series of images which would make it
possible for him to sense the nature of Kjell's revelation, and the
emotional effect of the scene is weakened by this failure. What
is best in Vesaas' portrayal of Kjell is the way in which, with a
small child's sharp perception of the grownup world, he understands the nature of the conflict between his parents:

He is six years old and has begun to take part in the concerns
which present themselves. He can see from his mother that something
is wrong. She is so busy arranging sheets and all sorts of linens, but
he can see that she is merely pretending today: she takes the neatly
ironed piles out and puts them back exactly as they were. Kjell can
see that everything is fine as it is, that she is doing it just to have
something to do.[3]

It is his sensitivity to the situation around him which leads to
his withdrawal, but which also makes it possible for him finally
to break out of his isolation. Although it is imperfectly realized
in *The Black Horses*, this motif of retreat from, followed by return to, life is one of Vesaas' most important themes, and the portrait he gives of Kjell serves as a good introduction to his later
more successful and convincing uses of it.

II   The Bell in the Knoll

In 1929 Vesaas published his first collection of short stories, *The Bell in the Knoll* (*Klokka i haugen*), written in London during the summer of 1928. He had written and published a number of prose sketches and short stories before this, and although several of them had also appeared, usually in somewhat altered form, as chapters or episodes in his novels, they had not been collected and published separately. All seven stories in *The Bell in the Knoll* were written expressly for this collection, which represents, in general, a clear step forward in his development as an artist, and it was also the first of his books to be translated into a foreign language.[4] Only one of the stories in the collection is obviously modeled on the work of another writer—"Dead Cat Pond," which belongs to the type of satirical study of Norwegian rural life brought to perfection by Hans Kinck—and even that is a quite acceptable example of the genre. Of the remaining six, two are nature and animal studies (the best of these, "Before Rain," has been mentioned in Chapter 1), two are perceptive stories about children and one deals with a slow-witted farm hand. The remaining story, "Signe Tone," is the best of the stories in the collection, and illustrates well the extent to which Vesaas was developing as a writer.

The opening sentence sets the mood:

> One morning there was a rainfall so light that it could better be called a fine mist; it seemed to come from nowhere, just filled the air on all sides.[5]

A road running through a farm landscape is described in a few sentences. A girl is walking along the road:

> The misty rain was good to her: she welcomed it as the countryside around her welcomed it, and grew lush beneath it.
> If she didn't realize it herself, there were many who had already taken stealthy note of the fact that she was soon to be a bride.[6]

She walks through the woods and feels not too safe, but it is nothing compared to how she feels when she approaches the row of farms she must pass to get home:

> And then it *was* unsafe, fateful, as when one hears the bell in the knoll! It was when she had come far enough to see the cluster of farms.

Saw the farms. For she felt acutely that I will live on one of them, all my days. Some fellow will fetch me and renew the vitality in one of them, through me.[7]

She feels the threat from the farms as she passes:

It was the ancient farm itself which blinked with its green panes of glass, and thought:
You will be a good wife for our son, it blinked pensively. And he will need all you can give, because he will have to toil endlessly. And you will have to toil. . . . She walked slowly on. The heavy fragrance of unmown meadows closed in around her. Everything was pungent and well-developed and ready.
Farm after farm was left behind, but had long since taken note of who was passing; she would never escape from them alive. The precious blood of new people was needed. An old farm always has young women in mind.[8]

The emphasis in this story is in the creation of an atmosphere—an atmosphere of maturity and ripeness and the inexorable workings of fate. "The bell in the knoll," a reference to old Norwegian folk beliefs in supernatural beings dwelling in the hills, which the workings of fate are likened to, is an image of everything that is unknown, hidden and uncontrollable, and expresses Signe Tone's feeling of helplessness and insecurity in the face of the fate she knows will be hers. Thus she finds herself in essentially the same position as Toremun in the Grinde novels, but there is an indication here that her final acceptance of her fate will be a happy one.

III   *The Dyregodt Tetralogy*: Father's Journey

In the fall of 1929 Vesaas, having returned to Norway, set out on the most ambitious writing project of his career: the series of novels about Klas Dyregodt. Originally intended as a trilogy which was published in three separate volumes between 1930 and 1932, it eventually consisted of four volumes, the final volume following in 1938. The entire work consists of nearly 1,000 pages, and demonstrates quite conclusively that a large, epic novel is not well suited to Vesaas' style. It is repetitive and at times annoyingly static, but nevertheless occupies, along with the two novels about Per Bufast published in 1934 and 1935, a central position in Vesaas' work. The problems and conflicts which

Klas and Per face in the course of the novels about them seem to parallel quite closely the problems and conflicts of Vesaas' own life up to that point, and the resolution of which appears to have been necessary for Vesaas' development as an artist.

The strongest impression the reader receives from the Dyregodt novels is that of the landscape, which plays a unifying role in the structure of all four novels. The locus of all the action throughout the entire series is a long valley dominated by the river running through it. The action takes place at four stations along the valley, from a farm at its uppermost end to a town located where it meets the sea, but revolving around a point at the approximate middle of the valley. At this point there is a dam which controls the level of the lake behind it and supplies the water needed by a sawmill in the town at the mouth of the river far below.

Klas, the central character of all the Dyregodt novels, is a foundling who was raised by a cabinetmaker who lives in the valley below the dam, about halfway between the dam and the sea. One day his foster-father tells him that he has to go to Dyregodt to be assistant to the man who tends the dam there, Aslak Dyregodt. Klas is both puzzled and angered by this. When he protests that tending the dam is no concern of his, he receives the cryptic answer: "Oh, in one way or another it is a person's concern. You may understand that someday."[9] At this he resigns himself to the situation:

Klas felt like rebelling, but his courage failed him. He understood that he was a pawn in a game.[10]

Klas's feeling that he is the helpless instrument of an inexorable fate grows steadily stronger as he finds out more and more about who he is. It turns out that he is the son of Aslak Dyregodt by a young girl who drowned herself in the river after bearing him. Aslak has no children with his wife, Såve, but three outside of the marriage. The dam is old, and trembles under the pressure of the huge mass of water behind it, and Aslak is on the point of breaking under the strain of tending it. He lives in a state of "walled-in dread,"[11] fearing that he will one day lose control of himself and open two slime-covered bottom sluices which could bring on the catastrophe that everyone living in the valley below the dam fears. Aslak also sees the pressure of the water against the dam as an expression of the pressure on his conscience of the

sins he feels he has committed, and is convinced that someday it
will destroy him. When Klas finally realizes what the weight of
responsibility is doing to his father, he loses all hope, and imagines that he, too, is fated to be destroyed by the river. But Aslak
as a literary figure is more than just a picture of the destructive
forces innate in human nature; he is also invested with a great
love of life, which he attempts to pass on to his son. Aslak, before
he became trapped by his feeling of dread, had worked the farm
at Dyregodt, and speaks one day to Klas about the earth:

> "Do you realize what soil is, Klas?"
> "No."
> "Good soil is full of life." He bent down and picked up a handful.
> "There's so much tiny life in it that it's completely alive." He let the
> earth run through his fingers. . . ."You have to bring about growth,
> if you want to be allowed to live yourself," Aslak said.[12]

When spring comes Aslak tells Klas that he must go to Stallbrokk, one of the uppermost farms in the valley, to stay with his
grandmother, Sigrid Stallbrokk, who has now been told of Klas's
existence. This time Klas follows the order with no thought of
rebelling, convinced as he is of the futility of fighting against
what is fated to be.

He sets out immediately, but is delayed on the way. He meets
a team of log drivers, one of whose members has been killed in an
accident. They ask Klas to sit with the body, which is lying in a
dilapidated hay barn nearby. Klas sits with the body for two
days during which time it rains constantly. The second night he
dreams that Aslak comes to him and tells him to return to Dyregodt because of the danger of the dam breaking under the weight
of the rising water. Klas returns. A gang of men works feverishly
to strengthen the dam. At one point in the night there is momen-
tary panic when it appears the dam is about to break. Aslak has
a heart attack and dies. "Had father traveled his journey to the
end, or had he just now set out?"[13] is the question Klas asks himself at the end of *Father's Journey*, the first of the Dyregodt
novels.

Father's Journey (*Fars reise*) is in many ways a remarkable
book. It is written in a much more concentrated style, with more
consistent and effective use of ellipsis and short, abrupt sentences
than any of Vesaas' earlier novels. This contributes greatly to the

overall effect, which lies in the atmosphere of tension and foreboding that is built up around the central image of the dam. This
atmosphere is intensified by the frequent repetition of the words
"Feel the trembling!" They refer to the trembling of the dam beneath the weight of the water, and serve almost as a refrain
throughout the novel.

The characterizations are much more convincing than ever before. Aslak is a complex person, puzzling but believable, and in
the figure of Klas Vesaas presents a picture of adolescence at its
most fearful and hesitant. Once more these characters find themselves at the mercy of powerful forces outside them, but there is
a hint here that there may be a way out for Klas. The dam,
frightening as it is, seems to extend a challenge to Klas, but one
that he does not yet seem to be ready to meet.

The imagery in this novel is more unified and effective than
in any of the novels which preceded it. Besides the landscape
and the dam, the main interest centers around a motif that returns often in Vesaas' later writing: that of empty hay barns. In
the final section of the novel Klas watches over the dead body of
the log driver in such a barn, but even more important is a group
of hay barns standing on the bottom of the reservoir:

> They had been too worthless to move, and their timbers were too
> moldy and mildewed to float. When the water level was low they ap-
> peared above the surface, meaninglessly standing there in the mud,
> without roof or ridgepole.[14]

Their threatening presence, even when they are not visible or
when no mention is made of them, is one of the most important
elements of the atmosphere surrounding the dam and the lake
backed up behind it.

IV *The Dyregodt Tetralogy:* Sigrid Stallbrokk

The second novel in the series, *Sigrid Stallbrokk* (1931), is
considerably weaker than the first. After his father's death, Klas
goes to live with his grandmother at her farm. The description of
the old woman and the farm is intentionally grotesque, but the
effect is often exaggerated. Sigrid has given up all hope since the
news of the death of her daughter reached her. Thinking that
her daughter's unborn child, which would have continued the
family line, has died with her, she has let the farm fall into a

state of disrepair and she herself has turned to drink. Meeting
her serves to reinforce Klas's feeling that he, too, is doomed, and
he becomes more despondent than ever. Sigrid has no hope for
herself, but sees Klas as an instrument to continue the family line.
She tries to force him and Eli, a girl who works for her, to have
a child together. At first they resist, since they do not love each
other, but finally succumb to what they feel is their fate. Sigrid
has taken to singing in the evenings when she is drunk, a song
"resonant and wild,"[15] and this has a frightening, hypnotic effect
on Klas and Eli. Once more the image of the empty hay barns is
used. When Eli and Klas break under Sigrid's will they are hiding from her in such a barn, and the overtones of hopelessness
are strong:

> The barn resembled a creature emptied of all strength and contents
> and life, which now can only open its lips to yawn as darkness falls.[16]

Later, after it is clear that Eli is pregnant, a windstorm blows
the barn down, and the farmhouse creaks ominously. Both Klas
and Eli feel there is no hope for them; they cannot love each
other and are doomed to die. Eli leaves Stallbrokk, and both Klas
and Sigrid are afraid that she, too, has drowned herself in the
river. But they receive the message that she has gone to Dyregodt
to bear her child. Klas stays at Stallbrokk until Sigrid dies.

V   *The Dyregodt Tetralogy*: The Unknown Men

The third novel in the series, *The Unknown Men (Dei ukjende
mennene)*, continues this mood of despair and hopelessness. After
the death of Sigrid, Klas goes to live with his half-brother Pål
Tun, who owns the sawmill at the mouth of the river. Word is
received that Eli's child was stillborn, and that she has left
Dyregodt. Thoughts of death are uppermost in Klas's mind, and
he has to be forcibly kept away from the whirring saws in the
mill. His despair is so total that when he sees a dead thrush he
takes it as an omen. He has had the submerged barns in the
reservoir at Dyregodt constantly in mind, and he decides to go
there and kill himself, thus surrendering to what he feels is his
unavoidable fate and completing the pattern of self-destruction
set by his father, mother, and grandmother.

He is thwarted, however, in his purpose by the gentle but
forceful intercession of Såve Dyregodt, Aslak's widow. When he

arrives at Dyregodt, Såve guesses his purpose for coming and tells him, simply and quietly, that he is the master of his own fate. He dismisses her words, determined to go through with his plan, and rows out to the hay barns, which are standing clear of the water:

> He waded up to a gaping door. Don't look at this building—this is just the *place*—I've simply come to where I belong. An acrid odor filled his nostrils when he stood at the door opening, and his feet were stuck fast. He stood there for a while with one foot on each side of the threshold, and could get neither free. The threshold was so high that it was clear of the mud. Klas pulled his foot loose and entered.
>
> There was also an opening on the opposite wall. A window. Fallen rafters and ridgepoles leaned against the walls. Everything was covered with dried mud.[17]

Klas is about to hang himself when something happens:

> He looked up. Yes, the sun was shining. It was just beginning to pale, shaded by a mountain somewhere. At least I've had a chance to see the sun, he thought, and walk on grass—. He repeated it to make it clear to himself. Grass—.
>
> You're the master of your own fate, Klas.
>
> He started. In spite of everything, his sight was blurred now. Then this filled his ears: You're the master of your own fate. They sounded clearly, it seemed to him: the words which Såve Dyregodt had spoken a little while before. In a sudden flash he saw her before him: weary, and strangely radiant, half departed, engaged in a quiet, desperate struggle against death and destruction—a sudden flash, then he again saw only slime and rot.
>
> But her words remained before him, as if written on the wall: you're the master of your own fate; they cannot drive you into death. They are gone.[18]

He still tries to resist the power of her words, but in vain:

> But he had been wakened now, now that a faint hope was in sight, and new thoughts raced through his mind: *It wasn't true that this was fated!* An avalanche can be stopped. . . .
>
> He thought bluntly: I won't. Lying here in the mud is much too despicable a thing. I must be worth more than that.[19]

Klas returns to Dyregodt, determined now to defy the forces which had drawn him to the submerged barns and thoughts of self-destruction. When he returns, Såve is dead:

Was there a connection? He had left her trembling from exertion, he left her to make an end to himself, do it despite her silent struggle against it. She was helpless, because he too had to decide his own fate. Had it killed her?[20]

Despite Såve's death, Klas is still filled with hope because of the decision to live that he has made. He still feels cut off from other people, but something else starts happening within him:

Something began rising up on the horizon, something called responsibility. How is it to be borne? People do seem to be able to bear it.[21]

The whole question of responsibility is brought home to Klas by his observation of how the responsibility of tending the dam has affected the two men who had taken over after Aslak's death. They are Olav and Jörgen, who worked the farm for Aslak, and who have continued working the farm while tending the dam. Throughout the three novels they have represented a steadying, positive force, closely allied with the soil, the progression of seasons and everything that grows. They are calm and unswerving in their faith in life. Now Klas notices that even they have been affected by the pressure of the responsibility of tending the dam, and are no longer so sure of themselves. Exactly what the responsibility for the dam implies is not clear to Klas until one day he and Olav and Jörgen are on the dam together. They are looking out over the beautiful fields below them, when suddenly:

Klas cried out. Stood there with rolling eyes, pointing: "Look!"
At the end of the dam where the timbers met the supporting wall a thick, gushing stream of water was pouring out between the timbers and the wall.[22]

They all stand paralyzed until suddenly Olav jumps into the water and plugs the hole with his body. Klas and Jörgen run to the sluices to tap water out:

They ran back to where the leak was, and the knowledge of what it meant to tend the dam at Dyregodt cut through Klas like lightning. What was demanded.[23]

The water is tapped out, the dam repaired, and Olav buried. Klas and Jörgen wonder if they could have done what Olav did. Klas realizes how little he has known Olav, and Jörgen, too. They are "the unknown men" of the title of this third volume of the series. Klas makes a final trip to Stallbrokk, which is now deserted, and having thus completed his wanderings in search of his identity, returns to Dyregodt, aware that he must take over the responsibility of the dam. Eli visits to tend to the grave of their dead child, but Klas still feels no love for her, and she leaves again. He takes charge of the dam, not gladly, but satisfied that he has found his place in life.

The *Unknown Men* is an extremely important work within Vesaas' canon. In many ways the episode in which Klas is prevented from committing suicide by Såve's words is the key to an understanding of his entire production. From this point in his production on, the workings of blind fate are assigned a less prominent role and the question of human responsibility becomes the dominant theme, in one form or another, in nearly everything Vesaas has written. It is easy to see Klas as a step forward from Toremun Grinde, who was also faced with the problems of finding out who he was and how he should deal with the powerful forces at work on him. Toremun never came to any clear understanding of either himself or the nature of his relationship to the destructive forces in the world, and Klas is also very near to capitulating to the mood of despair and anxiety which had claimed all his closest relatives. The manner in which his salvation is effected is also typical for Vesaas. He is saved by his own efforts, but is aided by the timely intercession of another person. This motif, so basic to much of Vesaas' later writing, occurs as early as in *Children of Man*, when Knut Heddejor goes out in the middle of the night to prevent a young couple from committing suicide, but it is first in *The Unknown Men* that it is placed in a context in which the implications in terms of human responsibility are clear. The stages in Klas's development are also clear: first self-discovery, then acceptance of responsibility for himself, then a gradual awakening of his feeling of responsibility toward others. When *The Unknown Men* ends he has still not solved his problems of his relationship to others, but he has hesitantly accepted the challenge which the dam, and life, place before him.

The novels about Klas Dyregodt are, however, more than the story of a young man's awakening to himself and his responsibilities toward others. They can also be read, without placing any unnecessary strain on the imagery in them, as a discussion of the impending international catastrophe in Europe in the 1930's. The

central image of the dam also plays the main role in this respect.
Not only the possibility of a catastrophe if it breaks, but also its
constant trembling under the pressure of the water behind it,
underline this aspect of its significance. Some sort of trembling
or another is frequent in Vesaas' writing as an image of war or
the danger of war, and would seem to have its origin in an early
impression of world War I:

> And then it was 1914. I was seventeen years old. Great celebra-
> tions (on the occasion of the centennial year of the Norwegian con-
> stitution) had been planned for the summer, but the World War
> broke out in August. News of bloodbaths worse than anyone could
> imagine. It made an ineradicable, burning impression on those who
> experienced it. During the first months the ground sort of trembled
> beneath one's feet—even if it was all happening so far away.[24]

The question of responsibility in connection with war was also
on Vesaas' mind rather early. In an article written in Munich in
March, 1926, he asks:

> Won't the loser [of a war] ever be mature enough that he won't,
> after his defeat, live only to get revenge, and can't the winner realize
> what a tremendous responsibility he has?[25]

In this same article, which is entitled "Poison in the Blood,"
he also wonders "Where does it have its roots, this dark stream in
the blood?" but it would still be a few years before Vesaas began,
in his writing, to try to uncover the roots of the destructive impulses in man. In the Dyregodt novels he is more concerned with
questions of not only national, but individual, responsibility in
regard to the problem of war, as will be seen when the fourth and
final novel of the series is discussed.

VI Ultimatum

Before that final novel was written, however, Vesaas published three more novels, a volume of short stories, and a play
which, although it was not published until 1934, following the
publication of his next two novels, had been written in 1932. It
is closely related in many ways to *The Unknown Men*, and discusses directly the problems of war which are only touched on
indirectly there. Entitled *Ultimatum*, it was written essentially in
September, 1932, while Vesaas was living in Strasbourg, partially

on the basis of notes made during the two previous years,[26] that is, while he was writing *Sigrid Stallbrokk* and *The Unknown Men*. A contemporary article, describing conditions in Strasbourg and the German town of Kehl across the river, gives a good picture of the influences on Vesaas during the writing of the play:

> Strasbourg is full of soldiers. There are large garrisons stationed here. And if you walk across the bridge, you come to the small town of Kehl, and the first thing you see in the streets is a flaming swastika. ...The newspapers on both sides of the river tell daily how blood-thirsty the other side is. Everything you read and see makes you discouraged and hopeless.[27]

The action of the play is a direct reflection of this tense atmosphere. Five young people are waiting for the news of a neighboring country's reaction to an ultimatum that their country has sent. The two main characters are Stefan, a young pacifist who dreads the approaching war, and Arnold, a young poet who looks forward to the war in idealistic expectation of the great deeds that will be performed in it. They struggle for the allegiance of a young girl, Maria, who loves Stefan, and is pregnant with his child, but who finally turns to Arnold, whom she feels can give her something positive to believe in during the coming conflict. Despite the dramatic possibilities in this material, the play is disappointingly static, and when it is compared with the Dyregodt novels, and above all with later novels and stories that treat the problem of war indirectly, the play would seem to indicate that Vesaas is at his weakest when he is discussing problems directly, rather than creating atmospheres which allow the reader to make his own associations. There is a failure to integrate ideas in a convincing manner that weakens the dramatic impact of the obvious pacifistic message, as for example when Stefan cries out:

> Will you never, never learn? You should let a *shriek* rise up so that the blood of those who are preparing our destruction would freeze in their veins![28]

In *Ultimatium* this presentation of the shriek that is necessary to awaken people to their responsibilities to mankind is merely part of an unfortunately undramatic discussion of the imminence of the catastrophe of war that fails to engage the reader. The use of the same shriek in "Three Quiet Men," on the other hand, is an

example of the more effective associative technique which Vesaas
later developed.

Technically, the play is both experimental and interesting.
The stage description at the beginning of Act I gives a good
example of this:

(A hot, humid day. A bench standing among leafy bushes. The
dark green leaves form a thick wall turned away from the direct light.
The word ULTIMATUM gleams against this half-dark surface, in tall,
narrow letters of light that is sometimes weak, sometimes bright. That
is, just as this word pulses and scorches in the minds of all people
today.)[29]

Vesaas' use of this and other expressionistic effects in this play
was not especially fortunate. They are not successfully integrated
with the dialogue, which is basically realistic, and the overall
effect is strained. It is only to be expected that his acquaintance
with German expressionist theater in the period 1925-1932, when
he spent so much time in Germany, would have some influence
on his writing, but this influence was to appear in later prose
works in more successful forms than in this work for the stage.

VII   The Sandalwood Tree

In the spring of 1933 Vesaas returned to Norway, and his next
novel The Sandalwood Tree (Sandeltreet) was written that summer and published the same fall. This novel is the first of several
which reveal that Vesaas' attitude toward life had quite suddenly
and radically changed, nor is it necessary to search far and wide
for the cause of this change. In the fall of 1931, by this time more
or less resigned to being a bachelor for life,[30] Vesaas met the
poetess Halldis Moren, who was on her way to Switzerland. They
spent the following summer together in France and Switzerland,
and met again at Christmastime. What this experience meant to
Vesaas can be read between the lines in a poem (first published
in 1946) about that Christmas meeting:

... A train in the night. Tense, I stand and listen,
    as if waiting for a gentle call to come:
    A girl will soon be coming to Verona
    —and we will spend the holidays in Rome.

> Two shining bands of steel fade into the darkness
> out where the semaphores quietly play.
> Come, train. Come soon. I stare, enchanted, at the tracks:
> they quiver delicately now because you're on the way.[31]

The immediate effect of this total experience: falling in love,
engagement, eventually marriage and the establishment of a
family, was, as could be expected, to turn Vesaas' thoughts
toward the creative, life-affirming aspects of existence, though
at first glance the subject matter of *The Sandalwood Tree* might
seem to contradict this. It is a very simple story, almost decep-
tively so: a woman, happily married with two children ages ten
and eleven, becomes pregnant again. She has the presentiment
that she will die when she has given birth to her third child. She
tells her husband that before she dies she wants to see as much
as possible. He mortgages their house, and the entire family sets
out. Their money eventually runs out, but they continue their
wanderings, occasionally stopping to work to make money to
continue. At the end of the summer the mother gives birth to her
child, and dies.

As macabre as it might sound, *The Sandalwood Tree* is in fact
a strongly positive, beautiful book. The mother's death is no
tragedy, because in it there is an affirmation that life will continue. Vesaas carefully prepares this final effect by the selection
of images in terms of which the family's wanderings are expressed, and by the unusual, evocative name he allows the two
children in the family to bestow upon the coming baby: Livind.
No explanation is given as to how the woman might be able to
be so sure that she will die, and none is necessary. She recog-
nizes that death is a necessary part of life, and bows before this
fact. But although she is fated to die, she is in close contact with
the forces of life:

> The entire world was growing, and there walked mother and was
> not different from the blades of rye or the potato plants. Invisible
> threads extended from her toward everything she encountered, and
> from all of it she was creating Livind inside of her.[32]

Most of the impressions and images to which the family, and
the reader, are exposed are taken from life in the country. The
very first impression can be taken as an example. As they set out,
on foot, to walk to the station from their home in the country,
they pass fields:

There were fields on both sides of the road. Expansive fields with horses moving slowly along dark furrows. Large crows flew up and fluttered down again. The smell of earth and manure was carried on the wind. Mother breathed deeply. She wanted to gather in *everything*. The air was filled with the sound of an invisible chorus of birds. Mother listened. A steaming plow horse was standing close to the fence, taking a precious moment of rest. It didn't look up at those passing, but Mother also looked at *it* as she slowly passed.[33]

They travel by train and by boat and by car, they visit towns and also the capital city of Oslo where they, most appropriately, see a performance of *A Midsummer Night's Dream*. As time passes, the rest of the family gradually learns to see things with the mother's eyes:

"Did you get your eyes opened now?" Mother asked. And that's just how it was: they saw it with her eyes, had a veil drawn aside. . . . It felt as if they had been given a new sense, weak though it was.[34]

Two recurring images dominate the book. One is the central image of the mother as a tree. When she is depressed, thinking about her approaching death, she is "like a tree which a flock of black birds would soon settle in."[35] But in her lighter moments she has "shaken her tree free of birds."[36] She is no ordinary tree, however: "She was an unknown sandalwood tree to them, filled with foreign fragrance, and homeless."[37] Later on in the book, the image ceases to be merely an impression and becomes reality:

She *was* a tree, weighed down by its own fruit, and drawing into itself both heaven and earth. The three of them sat and were the fence around her garden. There was mist around her crown.[38]

As they protect her, she also protects them:

The branches of the tree spread out and formed a roof to be under. In spite of everything, they lived beneath *her* tree. There would be a crash when the tree fell, and soughing before the crash.[39]

The other recurring image is that of the plain, and is associated with her feelings toward her coming death. This image appears frequently in later works, and is a natural image of what is dreaded by a person born and raised surrounded by hills and mountains. In Vesaas' most recent collection of poetry, *May Our Dream Stay New* (*Ver ny, vår draum*, 1956), there is a poem entitled "The Plain" which expresses clearly this instinctive fear of the plain:[40]

> Blinded by the night, we stare before us.
> The plain which has stopped us
> expands in our thoughts.
> No comforting ridges any longer,
> only the plain in all its annihilating majesty.

But there is also in this poem, as in *The Sandalwood Tree,* a clear statement of how man must face death:

We will stand the sight of that mighty plain!

The other members of the family sit with the mother when she is depressed, and participate in her dread:

She took them with her out onto the desolate plains where she was roaming—and out there each of them felt he was alone. Each was lonely there. . . . It was horrible, and they ran and ran trying to find someone out on the mute plains, but each *was* alone. And mother was alone and cried out "Sit with me!" but they didn't see her and didn't hear her; *she* was on *her plains*—[41]

As her time approaches the mother's feeling of being alone increases. The family is separated at last when the mother lives at a farm waiting for the hour of birth, and death, to arrive, and the father and children live in a cabin in the woods nearby. The father and son are felling trees to earn their keep. This gives a clear forewarning of what is to come: "Trees fell with a soughing in their crowns."[42]

The baby is born, and everything appears to be all right, except to the father and children, who can see how close to death the mother is:

Margit did something that they remembered for a long time afterward. It was as if she became transformed as they watched. She embraced her mother and expressed so much love with her movement that Father and Egil were embarrassed, because they knew very well how totally Margit was exposing herself.

"I'm a girl too," she said, as the blood rushed to her face.

"Oh?" replied her mother. "You're still alone."

Father tried to pull Margit away, because this was surely too hard on her. She wouldn't budge.

"Tell me what it is!" she said to her mother, almost crying out.

Mother didn't answer.

"Mother—"

"It's all so boundless—" she said, and her eyes were mighty plains where no one could reach anyone else. Suddenly she straightened up and said clearly:

"Magnus! Go out for a little while; please go out all of you—I have to be alone—I don't want you to—"

They obeyed blindly. Told the other people in the house. Wandered around outside. But not for long. The woman of the house had gone in anyway, and now came out and called to them. But there was only peace in her voice.

They knew what they would find. They went in. It had been a hemorrhage.

But Livind was alive. He was sleeping, with a borrowed lace-trimmed cap pulled down over his head, sleeping with open mouth. Life had been stored up for him during the entire endless spring and summer. Now his bearer had passed on, while he slept unencumbered. Margit passed her finger lightly over his piteous brow, and cheek and chin. Her finger was a witching wand searching for hidden streams of vitality, friendship and kinship—that was Livind's consecration.[43]

In *The Sandalwood Tree* Vesaas approaches again and again the mystical, inexpressible aspects of life with open and unprejudiced senses, and demands of the reader that he do the same. If he does, he should be able to see this novel as one coherent, all-encompassing vision of the indissoluble bond between life and death. It is a book which, like the little children in the short story "The Vision," is illuminated from within by a miracle—the miracle of life: the constantly repeating cycle of birth, death, and rebirth.

VIII   The Great Cycle

This is also the theme of Vesaas' next novel, *The Great Cycle* (*Det store spelet*, 1934), this time in a more realistic, and for many people a more convincing, setting.

The Great Cycle is the first of the two novels which form the life history of Per Bufast. It follows his development from age six to his early twenties, and is essentially the story of his struggle to accept his role in life. It resembles in this respect the books about Klas Dyregodt, with the difference that by the end of *The Great Cycle* Per comes to a much more positive acceptance of his position in life than Klas does at the end of *The Unknown Men.* During his growing up, however, he feels the crushing weight of his lot in life to be just as oppressive as Klas does. Per grows up on a farm, with his parents, two brothers, and a maternal aunt whose presence plays a decisive role in his emotional development. His father is obsessed with the earth and the cultivation of it. He spends all the time he can clearing new land, to the extent that the rest of the family feels it is a mania. One day Per, with the bluntness of a six-year-old, asks his father if the earth is making him crazy.

> Father shot out an arm. An incredibly long arm. Per was seized in a tremendous grip. . . .
> He screamed in terror, "Let me go!"
> But no, he had it coming to him; he knew it would come. Father's grip, and his face, told him that something important was coming. Father said slowly, without letting him go:
> "You too will love earth, Per. It's all that matters."
> Per was trembling. He did not understand what Father was saying, but the words sank in. He would always remember them and the voice that spoke them: a voice full of dregs and rust because it was used so seldom.
> "You will love earth too, Per. When you're grown-up."
> "Let me go!"
> But those eyes were on his; he could not avoid them. Father said: "You will stay at Bufast to the end of your days."[44]

Per later comes to feel that with these words his father has passed sentence and placed a burden on him and his life,[45] and the words "You will stay at Bufast to the end of your days" serve as subtitle to the first half of the novel. The second half is subtitled "Bufast will give you all you need," but these words, also spoken by Per's father, represent no threat to Per since by the time they are spoken he is close to the point of being able to accept them, having already abandoned his plans to leave the farm. The development between these two states of mind is long and hard and is accomplished through a realization on Per's part of the close bond that exists between life and death. Per slowly comes to this understanding through observing not only the signs of life around him: the growing crops and animals and people, but also the signs of death which are ever present: the slaughtering of calves and cows he has grown fond of, the decaying of plants, the death of his younger brother Botolv in his presence, the shooting of the horses as they become too old to work. Per has difficulty understanding how his father can be kind to ani-

mals, as his aunt tells him he is, and still kill them. He finally
understands this when he himself has to take over the job after
his father has become too old to do it. Per has by this time decided to stay at Bufast to the end of his days, but he is not yet
really convinced that he loves the earth and that it will give him
all he needs. The long line of development is completed, however, after he has shot the old horse, Goldie, and is standing beside the carcass. In a vision that is one of Vesaas' most powerful
and moving he comes to an understanding of his role in life:

At that moment something mysterious happened. Per thought he
sensed the earth around him in a different way from before. The wet,
awakening earth had mild, cloudy air above it. A slight haze, a thin
mist, lay over the meadow. And here, in front of him, on this earth,
lay Goldie asleep forever. Per stood trembling and saw it all. He felt
that he loved earth. It awoke in his consciousness. He was completely
bound to it. To earth. His eyes had become clearer and his ears more
sensitive and his heart more open, it seemed to him. He stood in front
of the shot horse filled with one single emotion: he loved earth—and
air and water, and changes in the weather. It was *right* for him to
stay here to the end of his days.[46]

There is much more in *The Great Cycle* besides the story of
Per's acceptance of his position in life, however. There are many
fine descriptions of life on a farm, of both the joy and the hard
work that following the rhythm of the seasons brings with it, and
the development of a friendship between Per and a boy from a
neighboring farm, Olav Bringa, is sensitively portrayed. His feelings in this friendship are intermingled with his awakening sexual
feelings as he first draws close to and then drifts away from Åsne
Bakken. Åsne and Per first meet when they are both six years old
and bathing naked in the river running through the valley, in one
of Vesaas' very finest descriptions of the reactions of small children to the world around them. They later go to school together,
become confirmed together, but fail to develop a lasting bond
between them. Per's friendship to Olav is put to the test when
Olav and Åsne become engaged, and for a while he is isolated
and lonely. His aunt has married and is busy with her family, his
younger brother, Åsmund, has left the farm, his father dies, and
the responsibility for the farm falls on Per's shoulders. But he
discovers that he is not alone when Signe Moen, the sister of his
aunt's husband, comes to work on the farm one summer:

She was beautiful. But there was much else besides. She was quiet, he saw, and capable. Signe and Mother, and Signe and Aunt Anne together wove Bufast into a triple weave of womanly concern. The men merely went through and under the weave like a rough warp.

Later that summer he came to believe he had thought about her always. Ever since the day when Åsne had come wading down the river, naked and small, and had spoken the name Signe Moen for the first time.

One could not be killed. He had been dead inside since Åsne went to Olav. But it had been a delusion. He felt now that he was full of strength.[47]

The decisive event occurs one day Per and Signe are out raking hay together. They come across a frog that has been struck by a scythe blade:

The frog was injured horribly and lay struggling. Per shuddered. Then he said all of a sudden, "What shall we do with it? You, who are such a kind, kind person, shall we kill it?"

"Yes," she said seriously.

Afterwards he wondered why he had said such a thing. Calling her a kind, kind person. It sounded so odd, but it had simply rolled off the tip of his tongue.

He found a fence post to hit the frog. Signe turned away and bent to pick up another armful of hay. Per struck. The frog screamed a tiny scream the instant it felt the blow. Per heard Signe give a little moan when she heard the frog scream.[48]

Paradoxically, but in a way that is typical for Vesaas, Per is moved by Signe's compassion for the injured frog to declare his love for her. She responds calmly and matter-of-factly, which surprises him, but doesn't put him off:

He took her in his arms and held her close. She was fragrant with the earth and the moisture that had attached itself to her, and with her own youth. He felt her body rest against him. Her body was calm, as if arrived at its goal. A wry thought flashed through him: that she felt she had arrived at a goal of her own planning. No. He pushed it aside. She radiated calm and peace. But she could not blind him; he had gone through a hard apprenticeship in what work really is. He saw shadows in front of him: hard work, debt, anxieties. *But this is what I want.*[49]

The images of life and death and their interconnection return in the final paragraph of the novel and round off the story of Per's development toward maturity and responsibility:

He was close to the earth now, pressed close to it by the weight of a woman. He was intensely one with the great cycle.

Suddenly he remembered the dead figure of Goldie and how, close to that stiffened body, he had had his eyes opened to the chain of being. There was peace in pausing at the memory of Goldie lying on the trampled earth.[50]

IX   The Women Call: Come Home

In the second of the Bufast novels, *The Women Call: Come Home* (*Kvinnor ropar heim*, 1935), it is, as the title implies, the women who are in the center of the scene, continuing and developing a theme already stated in *The Great Cycle*:

Now he saw *Mother* better. She was always where she was needed, when clothes were torn and when any of them wanted food or drink. . . . Everything glided forward, interlocked as it was supposed to be, so that nobody paid any attention to it. . . . It occurred to Per that Mother did all this. The *days themselves* passed through Mother's hands and were ordered by her before they reached other people.[51]

In *The Women Call: Come Home,* however, there are other women in the foreground than Per's mother: Signe, Aunt Anne, and Åsne, surrounded by the seemingly limitless number of children they give birth to. Herein lies the main weakness of the book, which is best described in Vesaas' own words:

In the second volume about Per Bufast . . . the author seems to have been under the influence of some sort of childbed mania along with everything else, and the result was that there was just too much of a good thing. It probably happened that way because while I was working on the book a strange and exciting thought was constantly uppermost in my mind: at this very moment our first child is on the way–. The result was a lopsided book.[52]

But there are also many fine things in the book. Per's realization, as he grows older, that his children are just as lonely as he was as a child and just as much out of contact with him as he was with his father, is sensitively described. He realizes that he can do little to help them, but when he notices how they all long to leave the farm, he is gentler with them than his own father was with him:

"Well, I can tell you something: you will all soon love Bufast so much that it's frightening to think about."

He heard his own words. Heard how awkward they sounded. As if there was nothing to them. But he still saw how they were received and hidden away.[53]

The most remarkable figure in the book, however, is that of Per's old widowed mother, who more than all the others combined feels set aside and left out. Her old role has been taken over by younger women and her productive days are past. All she has left is her grandchildren, and her relationship to them is both strange and fascinating. The description given of her is startling and ominous:

She walked along among the bundles of drying grain, and was tall, dark, and slightly bowed—as are those for whom the grave has opened. She walked on the sharp grain stubble. That suited her. Dry stubble, and dead.[54]

She takes the smallest children by the hand and leads them around the farm:

The widow took the children with her and imprinted on their minds clear images of the farm. Often too overwhelming images for them to understand. She had a way of setting up such images. She would suddenly point at something and say sharply and harshly:
"Look at that!"
They started and looked. Looked in awe at what she was showing them. It bored into them because she said it in a special way and at the right moment.[55]

Per is not especially pleased at this activity, but realizes that his mother somehow has a right to do this:

Per knew also that he himself would imprint harsh images on their minds, and accompany them with harsh words. Had already done it, and would do it still more later. Their minds were open and receptive, so that inscriptions could be hewed in them, and there were many things on the farm which were as stern as hewn inscriptions.[56]

Maturity has also brought with it for Per an awareness of the rush of life in the world around him in which he takes no part: the sight of the ever-increasing number of automobiles passing on the road above the farm, the stories in the newspapers of war and unrest, of people coming and going while he remains always in the same place. The words "you were always in the same place" serve almost as a refrain throughout the book, but by the end of the novel, when Per is himself beginning to grow old (his first grandchild has just been born) he comes to an understanding of also this aspect of his life:

Per now thought that he saw things as they *were*. It was *not* frightening, and *not* bad to be always in the same place. You became indifferent to many things, and calm.[57]

Because of this emphasis on the importance of arriving at a calm and satisfied attitude toward life, *The Women Call: Come Home* is necessarily more static and less dramatic than most of Vesaas' other books. It is more repetitive and prosaic than *The Great Cycle*, and suffers by comparison with that novel.

X   The Clay and the Wheel

The following year, 1936, Vesaas published his second volume of short stories, *The Clay and the Wheel* (*Leiret og hjulet*). Most of the stories deal with various aspects of rural life, and two of them are closely connected with the Bufast and Dyregodt books.

"Twenty-one" is very similar in mood and theme to the final chapter of *The Great Cycle*. A girl is hired to help in the harvest on a farm, and the result is that she and the youngest son on the farm fall in love. The third day that they have been working in the fields together harvesting the mature grain is also his twenty-first birthday.

Then it happened, without warning, as if overwhelming, unknown forces were at work: *I* don't know how it happened, and probably never will understand it, but I was of age now, and Hild was in front of me, and I took three or four steps over to her without the others noticing. She was warm and her dress was open at the neck; she was tired, she was good—and what I did was strangely right and natural: I stretched out my hand and touched her arm. A shock ran through her. Two of my fingers lay against the curve of her arm. . . . And hardly knowing how it happened, I spoke the first, heavy words, quickly:
"Will you meet me by the big stone down there this evening after work?"
"Yes," she answered, confused.
"Yes," I said.[58]

In this story, as in *The Great Cycle*, the young people find their place in life through their close association with the forces of life and growth, and it is one of Vesaas' most poetic and evocative variations of this theme.

The story "Nils Fet" is closely related in its theme to the first of the Dyregodt novels, *Father's Journey*, although the details of its plot are quite different. It is, in fact, the reverse of the situation near the end of that novel, when Klas sits watch over the body of a dead log driver and waits for the man's relatives to arrive. Nils Fet is a sixteen-year-old boy whose father has been killed in an accident while working as a log driver. Nils has to travel up a "long and unknown valley"[59] to fetch the body. He trembles at the thought of the responsibility that has been placed on him as the oldest male in the family:

> Trembled because of something that he felt to be certain and unavoidable: He *had to* grow up quickly. What had happened would make his rapid growth necessary. Those at home would weigh heavily on him.
> *And he had to bear it.*
> Yes, I will—[60]

By the time he has arrived home with the body and has to face his waiting mother and smaller brothers and sisters he *has* begun to grow and is able to face his responsibility and shoulder his burdens.

XI *The Dyregodt Tetralogy*: The Heart Hears Its Native Music

At the end of *The Unknown Men*, Klas had begun to be aware of the problem of the individual's responsibility toward others, but without as yet being able to engage himself actively in the lives of others. He is still out of contact with life as he sits on the dam, even though he has accepted the responsibility for his own fate. In 1932 this seemed to Vesaas to be a fitting conclusion to the story of Klas, but the course his own life had taken in the intervening years caused him to change his mind by 1938:

> At any rate, a different wind was blowing now. The three-volume series about Klas Dyregodt couldn't be allowed to end in that depressing manner. The author decided that Klas just wouldn't have behaved like that. Therefore Klas was hauled forth again and thawed out so that he could discover life around him. . . .[61]

The result of expanding the story of Klas in this manner is a book which is poorly integrated with the three earlier works.

Despite several introductory chapters devoted to summarizing
the events of the first three volumes, the basic change in attitude
on the part of Vesaas seems to have made it impossible for him
to weld Klas's later development onto the description of his
earlier condition. The fourth volume is much longer than any
of the first three, is frequently tedious and repetitive, and makes
an overall weaker impression than the earlier volumes. It does,
however, add perspective to the problem of responsibility that
Klas had become aware of at the end of *The Unknown Men.*

When *The Heart Hears Its Native Music* (*Hjarta höyrer sine
heimlandstonar,* 1938) opens, Klas has been tending the dam
alone for a year. His feeling that he must do something to avert
the coming catastrophe grows stronger and stronger:

> For each week that passes he sees more clearly what he has to do.
> What is necessary. The dam either has to go, or be transformed into a
> mountain that *cannot* burst.[62]

A constant reminder of this responsibility is the memory of
Olav's sacrifice of himself, which Vesaas expresses in a beautiful
image. The memory of Olav

> is like a hidden tree that rises up from the dam at that spot. He
> sees a tree when he thinks about him. It will never wither. It is
> Olav's tree. And he who is the tender of the dam and sees it, trembles
> deep within him: see the hidden tree. The blind challenge. The in-
> human demand. The beautiful tree stands, its leaves motionless,
> blooming summer and winter.[63]

Klas lives up to this demand by forcing Pål Tun to build a
new dam. He threatens to stir up the people living in the valley
below the dam until they demand that a new dam be built.
Pål finally gives in, and the new dam is built, but at such a
great cost that Pål loses both the dam and the sawmill. The
new dam is solid and safe, and holds the water of the reservoir
without trembling. This only precipitates a new crisis in Klas,
however. Although he has now met what he felt was his responsibility and has succeeded in averting the disaster, he still finds
himself out of contact with life.

Once more another person speaks decisive words to Klas.
His foster-father is on his deathbed, and speaks to Klas of the
emptiness of his existence, and that he must become part of
life. Klas responds positively to this encouragement, and his

feeling that he is meant to live is strengthened: his heart hears music from its native land and he feels more strongly than ever that its native land is life.[64] This helps him to decide to get in touch with Eli, and they decide to marry and try to live together. They leave Dyregodt and move to Ru, where Klas was raised. Klas struggles to make a living at carpentry, and to learn how to love Eli. They have two more children, both of whom die, but these tragedies merely increase Klas's determination. He finally does feel that he loves Eli, their fourth child lives, and Klas at long last feels that he is part of life. The last sentence of the novel describes concisely his final state: "Now he is part of it all, like everyone else."[65]

In this fourth and final volume of the series Klas completes the long development from his original state of isolation and anxiety to one in which he feels that he is responsible for and involved in the lives of others, but this is not the only sense in which *The Heart Hears Its Native Music* can be said to be the end point of a long development. From both a stylistic and thematic standpoint Vesaas had developed fully as a writer by the time he had come to this point in his career. If this novel is compared with any of his first four novels the most obvious difference is its total lack of sentimentality. This change in attitude makes its appearance not only in the more restrained and terser style, but also in the treatment of themes. The difference in treatment, for example, of the theme of self-sacrifice is striking. The manner in which Olav's self-sacrifice, and the effect which it has on Klas, is described is totally devoid of the religious sentimentality that weakened the effect of this theme in both *Children of Man* and the Grinde novels. In the Dyregodt novels the necessity of self-sacrifice is a stern and unavoidable fact of life, and is tied in with the question of man's responsibility to his fellow man. Similarly, the rather romantic desire to do penance which was felt by many of the characters in Vesaas' earliest books has in his novels from the 1930's been transformed into a realistic willingness to assume the burdens of mature responsibility. Even the theme of longing for a better time to come has been tied in with the problem of responsibility which is central to both the novels about Klas Dyregodt and those about Per Bufast. In these novels, instead of longing for a better life in the future, the principal characters learn to accept their lives as they

are here and now, and to assume willingly the responsibilities
which this implies.

The transformation of the traditional religious themes of his
earliest writing into discussions of the overcoming of anxiety,
the discovery of the self, and the acceptance of responsibility
for oneself and others clearly reflects a change in Vesaas' own
attitude, one which is also apparent in the lack of direct expression of religious belief in his writing from *The Black Horses*
on. He allows both Per Bufast and Klas Dyregodt to express his
new attitude.

Per Bufast's adolescent struggle with the problems of God and
the Holy Ghost occupies a central position in the story of his
growing up in *The Great Cycle,* and the attitude toward religious
expression at which he finally arrives is concisely summed up:

He thought about God more shyly now. It was impossible to talk
about him. Ugh, the teacher at school who moralized and chattered
about Jesus as if it were an ordinary name passing his lips—this name
that Per found impossible to say unless ordered to do so, that he would
rather not even think about, he felt such respect and shyness toward
it.[66]

And in *The Heart Hears Its Native Music Klas* thinks:

You shouldn't shout about God; that's something to be kept to yourself, otherwise it ceases to be holy and ineffable and incomprehensible.[67]

This new reluctance to open and frequent mention of God's
name hardly represents, however, a turning away on Vesaas'
part from problems of a religious or ethical nature. Quite to
the contrary, it represents a much deeper respect for their
holy, albeit "ineffable and incomprehensible," nature than the
superficial outbursts of his earlier writing. The stories of the
developing maturity of both Klas and Per are to a very great
degree stories of development toward a deeply religious, ethical
attitude toward life, and Klas's attitudes in this respect, as they
are expressed in *The Heart Hears Its Native Music* when he is
at the end of his long wandering between the various stations in
his life, can undoubtedly be taken as expressions of Vesaas'
own attitudes at that point in his life.

The Heart Hears Its Native Music also gives a good picture
of Vesaas' thoughts and feelings about the increasingly threaten-

ing political situation in the world at the time of its writing. While Klas is still struggling with the problem of how he should fulfill his responsibility toward the people who live in the valley below the dam he wonders:

The thousands of people in the valley down below.—They know about this mountain of water. Feel the pressure of it. In all their worst moments they see it. See it burst.—Why don't they storm it like a raging army sometime it is empty, and tear it down bit by bit? No one says a peep about anything like that.... No one flames up in hatred against it, but all bear the nameless weight and pressure of it. It is never mentioned. Thousands of people are silent....[68]

One of Vesaas' most common images of catastrophe also makes its appearance here:

The dam is threateningly high. There is an abyss on its lower side.[69]

The abyss toward which the world was rushing in 1938 was World War II. It is possible to look upon the series of novels about Per Bufast and Klas Dyregodt as works in which Vesaas worked through and solved for himself many of the problems of his own life, and which needed solving before he could deal with problems of a broader social and moral nature. As oldest son on a farm he was faced with much the same conflict of interests as Per Bufast in *The Great Cycle,* and Klas Dyregodt's feeling of isolation paralleled his own condition during many years before 1932. The resolution of these conflicts, though to a certain extent in different ways than he allowed Per and Klas to resolve theirs, seems to have freed Vesaas to concentrate on other problems which had been of concern to him for many years. He was soon to turn his full attention to the problem of the origin of the destructive impulses in man which lead to war and which he had written about as early as 1926 in the article "Poison in the Blood" quoted earlier in this chapter. The years between 1938 and 1940, however, seem to have been years of hesitation and indecision for Vesaas. He worked on two plays, but discarded them both.[70] An essay written in 1939 reveals his thoughts in those years:

These are the new times: things move in closer and closer around us. And we who really need so much room.... What will happen to us then? No wonder we tremble before what we see approaching, we here in Norway, too. We'll probably not escape it either.[71]

The indecision and anxiety which Vesaas felt during these years were soon to be released, however, by the coming of the catastrophe which was in the background of so much of what he had written in the preceding decade. The German invasion of Norway in April, 1940, had an immediate and lasting effect on Vesaas' writing.

CHAPTER 4

The War Years and Their Aftermath
1940-1950

I The Seed

AMONG my books *The Seed* stands as a dividing line. It wasn't planned that way, but something so horrifying and unbelievable had happened that it simply brought with it a new way of writing. Not for the sake of any program, but just because it came by itself. Some sort of new way of reacting to things.[1]

The Seed (*Kimen*) is a novel in which the themes of doing penance and accepting responsibility are fused. The external plot deals with a murder and its aftermath. A mentally unbalanced man comes to a small, peaceful island, seeking peace and quiet. He accidentally witnesses an example of violent animal behavior, and this experience completely deranges him. He murders a young girl, Inga, whom he happens to meet, and is hounded and killed by the girl's brother, Rolv, and people from the neighboring farms. This action occupies the entire first half of the novel, but is itself merely an introduction to the true substance of the book: the problem of assigning responsibility for the killing of the deranged murderer. The father of the murdered girl, Karl Li, who was away from the island at the time, is adamant in his condemnation of the act of senseless vengeance: "Violence must not be tolerated,"[2] even though this judgment falls most heavily on his son, who was the leader of the mob that performed the act. In the second half of the novel, all who had participated in the killing come to the farm where the bodies of both the girl and her murderer lie, and hold watch in the barn during the night. Although they are all gathered together, it is a lonely watch: "Each of them had to account to himself, with no help from anyone else."[3] The emphasis throughout the novel is on the individual's responsibility to account for his own behavior and, although it is entirely possible to read it merely as a story of murder and vengeance on an out-of-the-way island, it is natural to see deeper implications in it. It was written during the summer of 1940, during the first months of Norway's involvement in World War II, and reflects vividly the mood of those months, expressing shock and despair at the extremes of brutality to which men can resort when caught up in mass hysteria of any origin, and condemning violence on both the individual and, by implication, national level.

In the first half of the novel an attempt is made to explain how such violent behavior is possible, by making an analogy with the behavior of animals. Two sows become frightened and begin to fight. They not only kill each other, but also frighten a younger sow which has just given birth to a litter. In her terror she begins devouring her young, and it is this act which in turn shocks the visitor to the island into insanity. Although this sequence is unconvincing as an explanation of the origin of human violence, it serves well as background for the story which follows. The parallels between animal and human behavior are underlined by a striking image, which is also the subtitle of the first half of the novel: "The Pit." It appears first in the description of the sows:

Long naked tusks protruded all too plainly from ugly jaws, vicious teeth rooted in flesh—beneath the pitted, narrowed, overhanging brows.[4]

It also appears in the description of the boar in his pen, as he tosses a stone into the air:

The stone fell back onto his skull. Into the hollow pit beneath the overhanging brow. Thud—into the dark pit.[5]

The image is expanded when the sows become frightened:

It grew dark about them. The pits in their brows deepened. . . .
Thud.
Not from outside, as when the boar was struck by the stone, but from inside.
Thud—down into the abyss. To the doomed and lost. Into the dark pit.[6]

The image of the pit is later carried over to the people chasing the murderer: "They were all headed for the deep pit within themselves."[7] After the killing the image is expanded still more:

Something moves at the bottom of the pit. Mangled. Crawling.
Oppressive silence. Wakening voices deep down inside one's soul.
Take care, they say.
Who are you? they seem to ask.
You try to move, and begin lying to yourself: I had no idea. That's
never happened to me before.
The voices answer: you know you're lying. The pit is in your brow.

You look at yourself, and see within yourself a sweeping landscape
with vast plains and wooded mountain slopes capped with flying
clouds. But you also see treacherous hidden pits, to be skirted and
avoided. There are unknown things concealed in their depths. Let
them lie there. No one shall know about them.
Let them lie at the bottom of the sea.—
A voice breaks through:
There'll come a day when all that—
No, never! you answer hastily, desperately. But that insistent voice
cannot be stilled.
There'll come a day when the sea within you shall give forth all
that lies hidden in it now. Your own tiny, deep, ugly sea. Its bottom is
turbulent and slimy and murky. Watch yourself!
You shove it away angrily and answer boldly: I'm not afraid.
You never figure on the slide, the avalanche that can sweep all be-
fore it and expose the landscape as it really has been all along.[8]

In this passage a number of important motives are brought
together in a single image in which the human personality is
compared to a landscape. Both the reference to the avalanche
which sweeps all before it and the earlier reference to the abyss
serve as points of connection with the theme of impending
disaster in the Dyregodt novels. The abyss referred to here can
be seen as being identical with the abyss on the lower side of
the dam at the beginning of *The Heart Hears Its Native Music*,
and the avalanche is the same avalanche that Klas discovered
could be stopped in *The Unknown Men*. In the Dyregodt novels
the avalanche was stopped again and again, the destructive
forces within man were held in check, but in *The Seed* the
avalanche is loosened. The parallels with the international political situation in both cases are obvious.

The Seed is more than a pessimistic statement of the presence
of destructive forces within the human personality, however. It
is also a determinedly optimistic statement of faith in the ability
of man to rise up again after defeat and degradation, presented

in the second part of the novel, subtitled "The Seed in the Dust."
After the night spent in the barn the islanders are able to face
themselves and their responsibility:

It became so light that the people were driven out of the barn
which no longer contained what they needed. It stood there towering
above them, used up and extinguished. They came out one after the
other. . . . A morning breeze stroked them gently. They shivered,
fragile as leaves. They had suffered much—but had risen to their
feet again.

A woman's voice said, to them all:

"Look: the island is as green as ever!"

It was Gudrun again, she who was carrying a child within her. She
needed to affirm that life would continue.

Yes, they saw it, all of them, and paused while it took hold of them
and brought things forth in them. It was so light now that they could
see clearly. The island was green. Karl Li's orchard was just as fertile
and generous as ever. It was only they who had been cast to the
ground.

But they had been able to rise up again. There must have been a
seed in the dust that had grown to strength and hope within them.
Their eyes cleared, they saw how steady in its course runs that which
calls forth life and death. The sun would return, and the grass and
leaves were green. It was God's greeting to the frightened and
tormented.

They stood shivering in the breeze, and saw what they had to do:
return to their accustomed places, and remember what they had settled within themselves that night. The island is ours, and it is green.[9]

It is typical for Vesaas that his agent for expressing faith in
the positive aspects of life is a pregnant woman. Another familiar
Vesaas motif also makes its appearance toward the end of the
novel. While the islanders are still in the barn, struggling to
accept their nature and their responsibility and to reaffirm their
faith in life, the black mare that belongs to Jens, who works Karl
Li's farm, comes stomping through the barn. Rolv Li starts up at
the sound:

It was the horse. Now he could see the outline of the animal in the
growing half-light. Soon after he felt Black Lady's breath against his
face and a firm, friendly nose nudged at him, accompanied by the
fragrance of green hay and oats.

It had such an immediate comforting effect on him that he could
somehow hardly believe it was true. It was like a reminder that life

would continue, and wanted all to participate. Then Black Lady stomped on through the barn and sniffed in wonder and friendliness at someone else.

Jens must have let Black Lady out, as a sort of conclusion to his period of penance in the stable. He had found help for himself, and therefore let the mare out to others.

Jens himself was not to be seen. But Black Lady came tramping through the barn and brought with her memories of innumerable days filled with work and the squeaking of wagon wheels and the smell of the sun on old harness. It was strange, but the smell of Black Lady reminded them first and foremost of the sun. It came as a greeting from God and an exhortation once more to take heart and carry on. Because everything around them carried on.[10]

It is natural that odors and sounds play an important role in this section of the novel, since the action takes place in the darkness of the barn during the long night of self-searching, but one important Vesaas motif appears in necessarily visual form: that of the contrast between light and darkness. Making use of one of his most beautiful images Vesaas describes how Inga's mother lights up her room, where her body has been placed, and the impression it makes on those doing penance in the dark barn:

There were many candlesticks on the old farm. She placed them around in the room. Her husband looked at her in amazement when he saw how she seemed in this way to lift the room up out of misfortune. That simple room with its pale walls. It was as if these walls were as thin as leaves and the room was floating away like a ship with its cargo.[11] . . .

From the barn, with all its stalls and pens and burdens, the shining light up at the house took the form of a sight joyous almost beyond belief. An incomparable light streamed out from two windows, from the depths of a joyous, luminous ship sailing through the night.[12]

The connections between the use of this motif here and in the passages illustrating it quoted in Chapter 1 (the children illuminated from within in "The Vision," the use of candle imagery in *Huskuld the Herald* and "Three Quiet Men") should be apparent, but it also has a special function within the structure of *The Seed*. The sight of the luminous room, with its message of relief from misfortune and burdens, serves as a presentiment of the return of the light of the sun the following morning, as does also the description of the smell of the horse.

This careful preparation of the reader, as well as the universality and utter simplicity of the image of the returning sun, is what makes the final scene of the islanders' reaffirmation of their faith in life such a moving and convincing one. Evocative repetition and simplicity of imagery are two of the most important elements of Tarjei Vesaas' style, and nowhere in his production are they illustrated more clearly than in this final section of *The Seed.*

This novel is also noteworthy for the appearance in it of a tendency in Vesaas' writing toward abstraction in character portrayal. In his writing before 1940 his characters are best taken at face value; even when they display unusual traits or attitudes they are best looked upon merely as individual human beings. In his writing since 1940, however, we frequently meet characters who must be looked upon as representing human types or isolated aspects of human personality or, in some cases, abstract concepts. A clear example of this in *The Seed* is the figure of Kari Ness. She is a widow, having lost her husband and two grown sons at sea. As a result, she has become a bit peculiar and has a habit of suddenly appearing when people least wish her to and of reminding them of what they should be doing. After the killing of the murderer she seeks out all who had taken part and calls them back to the barn. She clearly represents their consciences which are bothering them. What makes her most interesting within the context of a study of the development of Vesaas' literary techniques is her relationship to an earlier character in his writing. She is described in essentially the same terms as the widow in *The Women Call: Come Home:* she is "a tall, black-clad woman"[13] who wanders ceaselessly around the island confronting her neighbors, as Per Bufast's widowed mother wanders around the farm confronting his children with the sights of life. The two women frequently speak in the same curt, cryptic way, and the similarity of description is striking. The description of Kari Ness is, however, less strictly realistic than that of Per's mother; we know little about her and it is, as a result, not difficult to accept her as representing an abstract concept.

This is, of course, in keeping with the general nature of the works in which these characters respectively appear. Despite their many symbolic elements, the Bufast novels are basically realistic in tone and detail, while *The Seed,* despite its many detailed descriptions of real things and people, is basically symbolic in nature. The setting, the action, and some of the characters are clearly intended to represent something more than is contained in a strictly realistic interpretation. This was Vesaas' first serious attempt to break with the realistic tradition, and it is natural that it is not completely successful, primarily because the break was not clean enough. This shows up particularly in the first section. The parallel between animal and human behavior is somewhat labored, and the background of the stranger and his derangement is described in unnecessarily great detail. Since his role in the novel is only to serve as an impetus for the action, no purpose is served by the individualization of him as a character, and the result is merely a delaying of the progress of the action, and a weakening of the effect of the novel as a whole.

The Seed differs from all earlier Vesaas novels in another important respect. It is essentially dramatic, rather than novelistic, in construction. It respects the three classical unities of dramatic action: its action is limited to one location, that of the island, it takes place in the course of a single day, and it is not digressive. This is undoubtedly at least partially due to the fact that the original conception of the material was in dramatic form, even though it bore little resemblance to the final form,[14] but it also reflects a tendency toward concentration of action in his novels that began to appear in Vesaas' writing at this point. His next novel, *The Bleaching Yard,* was also conceived originally in dramatic form, and had actually been accepted for performance as a play in 1939 before it was withdrawn.[15] Although the novel was not published until 1946, it was written during the war, and stands in close relationship to *The Seed* both in terms of the problems discussed and the form employed.

II The Bleaching Yard

In *The Bleaching Yard* (*Bleikeplassen*) Vesaas continues his search for an explanation of the origin of violent impulses in man. In addition to the only partially successful comparison of human and animal behavior in *The Seed* there is also in that novel an indication that feelings of anxiety and isolation play an important role in the generation of these impulses. Not only does all the

action take place on an island, but there is relatively little close
contact between the characters in *The Seed,* even between members of the same family. Little emphasis is placed on this theme
in *The Seed,* but it is central to the action in *The Bleaching Yard,*
which is the story of Johan Tander, a man who feels out of contact with those around him and who is obsessed with murderous
thoughts.

The basic image employed in *The Bleaching Yard* is once more
the contrast between light and darkness. This manifests itself in
several ways. The unity of time is observed also in this novel, and
the action takes place during two evenings and the intervening
day, with much emphasis placed on whether it is light or dark so
that things can either be seen or are hidden from sight. It manifests itself also in the selection of the setting. The novel opens:

The white washing on the clothesline stands out against the darkness of the summer night by its own power. As if luminous. Exposed
to the dew tonight and to the sun tomorrow morning. . . .
It grows still darker. The light gradually fades. But it doesn't become pitch dark, and the linen in the bleaching yard can still be seen
glowing, like something which has a value all its own in the midst of
the eclipse of the night.[16]

The laundry to which the bleaching yard belongs is run by
Johan Tander, who now appears in the yard. The development of
the basic image continues:

He stands there in despair.
Cast light on me, he thinks, suddenly, at random.
Cast a little light.
Before it is too late.
Too late is a cruel phrase, and he stands still for a long time. Some-
where off in the darkness there is the rippling of water. The river flow-
ing past. It is so flat here that it flows gently, and can be heard only
when it is dark.
The undertow, he thinks.
He is caught in an undertow, that's what it is. One more dangerous
than the one in the river. When you're caught in an undertow you
suddenly discover it's too late. . . .
A wind is blowing in the stillness of the evening. No ordinary wind.
A hot, dark wind from the unknown valleys within oneself.
Cast a little light, he thought a little while ago.
Now he doesn't think that. He is standing in the wind.
Come—he calls to the wind. Come, wind.

Never stop, he thinks.
He stands there collecting the darkness around him. Near him the pale linen glows.[17]

The undertow Johan Tander feels caught in is the stream of destructive impulses he feels toward Jan Vang, a young forester who lives in the same building where his laundry is located. The immediate cause of these feelings is Tander's infatuation with Vera, a girl who works for him:

It had been going on for about a year. As long as Vera had been working at his counter. As soon as she came, it was as if a new room opened up within him. Unexpectedly and powerfully, like a revelation. Vera with piles of linen around her. Vera among the gleaming piles, always! *No one is allowed to enter here.* That's how it is. Just to look at and be near.
Don't go nearer. Something delicate would be crushed then. But no one else may either! he thought, blindly and desperately....
Then Jan Vang came, and it was not long before someone had entered the forbidden ring.—

The deeper cause, however, seems to be the loss of contact between Tander and his wife, Elise, although the reader is not given more than a hint of this:

[Elise] has noticed from his recent behavior that something is about to happen. Something has power over him. She can't ask about it, even though they have been good companions. There is something about this that holds her back.
Somewhere in the background there is a large, dark square hewn into what can be called the life that is past: their dead child. When it became apparent that there would be no more children, the whole thing developed into a large, dark square. But it is not so bitter now. It is something to be avoided, as one avoids dangerous hollows.[19]

This is the extent of the information the reader is given about the background of the situation he is presented with at the beginning of the novel, but it is in keeping with the sparsity of description in general. About Johan Tander, for example, we are told only that he is "a man about forty years old."[20] The characters in *The Bleaching Yard* are, in general, very little individualized, and the tendency toward abstraction in character portrayal apparent in *The Seed* is even stronger here. As a result it is at times difficult to see *The Bleaching Yard* as a direct representa-

tion of reality, although the behavior of the characters always
remains within the limits of what is possible, if not likely. It is,
however, a striking representation of the subconscious and incomprehensible (Johan Tander's own word for the effect Vera
has on him) forces at work in the human personality. The description of Tander's realization of his feelings for Vera as a revelation underlines the irrational aspects of the entire situation, as
does also another description of the washing hanging in the
darkness: "Over there the linen shone faintly, with magical
power."[21] The reader is carefully prepared in the opening pages
of the book to expect a story that will place great demands on his
powers of imagination and his ability to accept things that he
may have difficulty in understanding intellectually.

The first of these is Elise's attempt to help her husband. She
takes a piece of chalk and writes in large letters on a wall facing
their apartment: NO ONE HAS CARED ABOUT JOHAN TANDER.[22] It is
difficult at first to see how this could help him, and even Elise is
unclear about her motives for choosing this course. The immediate effect is that Johan's impulse to murder Jan is intensified,
since he assumes that it is Jan who has written the words. It also
increases the state of anxiety in which Jan lives, since he soon
learns that Tander suspects him and feels more strongly than
ever how Tander is after him. These increased feelings of fear
and isolation come close to breaking out into violence during a
meeting between Jan and Johan. They settle for threats at the
time, but both are sure that a showdown is coming. Before it can
take place, however, Tander discovers that it is Elise who wrote
the words on the wall. His reaction is spontaneous:

> His first reaction was one of violent rage—but it ended before he
> lost his head. The thought flashed through him how untrue it was,
> what she had written! Since it was she who had written it. She had
> done it to help him, however that could have been. She would not
> have exposed herself to this shame if she hadn't cared about him.—
>   What is written there isn't true.
>   He repeated it. It grew large before him, and became meaningful.
> *Elise did it out of concern,* as harsh as it is. Shamed herself to do it.
> How could she have had the strength?[23]

He feels relieved of the obsession that has had possession of
him, and realizes that he has been on the brink of insanity. He
hurries to tell Elise of the great change that has come over him,

but cannot find her. He talks to Vera instead and tells her that there is no longer any danger that he will harm Jan. As they are talking, Jan and two companions enter. They have been drinking together and talking about how they can protect Vera from harm. When they see Tander they decide to teach him a lesson and despite Vera's protests lead him out to "wash" him in one of his own laundry tubs. Although he is now changed, Tander realizes that he deserves it and goes with them quietly. What has started as a joke becomes deadly serious, however. The strain of everything that has happened is too much for Tander, and he collapses and dies as he is climbing up into the tub.

Parallel to this story of Johan Tander runs the story of Krister, an old man who feels he is about to die. He has for a long time been attracted to the bleaching yard and the clean linen there, although he can't quite understand why:

> If he had tried to explain why, it would just have come out non-sense. A large, large yard full of washed linen.—
> He had longed more than ever for clean linen last night. At one moment his heart was on the point of stopping, and the thought forced itself on him: *A clean shirt!* I have to have a clean shirt first. . . .
> I want to have a clean shirt on when I die. And I don't have one. But someone has to give me that shirt! For there's little time now.
> They'll give it to me at the first word. As soon as I open my mouth I'll get it. It's *different* today.
> I have to get a sign that I've *been* among people, that I haven't lived in vain. And that's the sign. I'll get that shirt at the first word.
> So I know that I've lived.[24]

Naturally, no one just gives Krister a shirt when he comes tottering pathetically along, neither Johan Tander nor anyone else he meets. They are either all too busy or don't believe him when he says he is about to die, and either say they will look into it or take care of it tomorrow. Krister finally *takes* a shirt off a clothesline, puts it on, and lies down to die in the bleaching yard. He then regrets having taken the shirt, and tries to take it off again, but the effort is too much for him. Krister, "who was alone in the world,"[25] dies. The parallel between the searches of Tander and Krister for someone who cared for them is completed when Tander's body is carried out from the laundry and placed in the yard:

Krister there, and Johan Tander here—their faces know no more obstacles, and rise up out of the dusk.[26]

The portrait of Krister is one of the most touching in all of Vesaas' books, while that of Johan Tander is one of the most disturbing. He is presented to us as a man who is gradually being driven into destructive isolation by forces he not only cannot control, but which he does not even understand. He seems to be trapped in a paradoxical state of anxiety in which he most fears precisely that which can save him, in this case close contact with another person. He has lost this contact with Elise, and is fearful of even trying to establish it with Vera, as is indicated by his looking upon her as something not to be touched, but only admired from afar.

This return to the "madonna" motif is not the only example of the appearance in *The Bleaching Yard* of motifs and themes from his writing during the 1920's. Tander's obsession and his will to do penance at the end of the novel remind one of Toremun in the Grinde novels, with the important difference that in Tander's case the psychological background for these states is much more convincingly portrayed. This is also true of Elise's will to sacrifice her own interest, "to shame herself," which is much better motivated in the novel than any of the examples of the will to sacrifice in Vesaas' earliest novels. Even the central image of the clean linen has a forerunner in Vesaas' writing in the 1920's. Lisle in *The Black Horses* flees from her feelings of having been debased in her unhappy marriage by sorting and handling her linens, but the effectiveness of the linen as a symbol of purity is much weaker in that novel than it is in *The Bleaching Yard*.

III   The Tower

In his next novel, *The Tower (Tårnet)*, also written during the war but first published in 1948 in a somewhat revised form, Vesaas continued his discussion of the dangers inherent in the state of human isolation. There are also connections between this novel and his earlier writing, but not so much in terms of themes as in the choice of setting and characters. As in *The Black Horses* the main action involves two families living in close proximity to each other, one a family of farmers who are in close contact with the earth and who have basically harmonious personalities, and the other a family which does not live off the earth and the members of which have basically neurotic personalities. In both novels the lives of the family of farmers serve as a background against which the tragedies which strike the other family are silhouetted. The "harmonious" family in *The Tower* is composed of Olav and Sigrid Sund and their three children, Jon, Astrid, and Björg, respectively 20, 17, and 12 years old. The farm is located beside a sound spanned by a long bridge. The farm is named after the sound, but the name can also be taken as a symbolic description of the psychological state of those who live on it and work it.

The other family consists of four people: Randolv and Jorunn and their two children, Nils and Vesla, ages 15 and 12. Randolv runs a garage located between the farm and the bridge. Both he and his wife are outsiders, both in the sense that they were both born and raised elsewhere, and in the sense that they keep to themselves. The personalities of the children have been affected by this, as could be expected:

> They were a bit different from the children over at the farm. Had a tendency to close themselves off and be standoffish.[27]

In the first chapter of the novel Nils is mixing ants from different anthills and watching them fight and kill each other. He knows that what he is doing is wrong, and he doesn't really want to do it, but he can't stop himself. He is plagued with feelings of guilt and anxiety because of it and these express themselves in an image:

> He saw it before him. Had himself formed it. An image:
> An invisible and yet shining tower, which the morning sun struck long before it reached down to us.[28]

Nils imagines that there is an eye in the tower watching him, and that something up there could crush him. It thus represents both his bad conscience and his fear of punishment.

At the beginning of the novel the family is in a state of change. Part of the nature of this change is clear: Jorunn is pregnant and will soon have her third child. All the members of the family are naturally nervous and restless because of this. There is some sort of change going on at a deeper level, however, and the nature of this is unclear. Randolv has recently stopped repairing

automobiles, leaving this work to two mechanics who work for
him, and instead he and Nils have begun tearing old automobiles
apart and selling the scrap. He is warned by one of his mechanics
that this destructive work can do damage to his soul, but he only
laughs. Something is happening to Vesla, too:

> She and Olav Sund had always been very good friends. Now they
> had started drifting apart, and it wasn't Olav's fault.[29]

The mood established in the first few chapters of *The Tower*
is one of foreboding, and it is not long before the tragedy strikes.
Shortly after the baby's birth Randolv and Nils, who are both
very fond of it, take it with them to the garage while they work
and set it near a pile of scrap iron out of the wind. When the
baby becomes sick they are quite sure it is because it had reached
out and stuck its finger on a sharp point on the rusty scrap. They
actually saw nothing, though, and tell this to Jorunn when she
asks, but they still feel guilty. Jorunn feels that they are hiding
something from her and begins to withdraw, both psychologically
and physically. After the baby dies, she breaks all contact with
them. She no longer eats with them, for example, but prepares
food and lets Vesla serve it. The situation places a psychological
strain on all of them, and they all become more and more withdrawn. Randolv and Nils become obsessed with the thought of
building up the pile of scrap to cover up the place where the
baby was injured. Nils begins to confuse the growing scrap pile
with the image of his invisible tower. Jorunn, for her part, becomes obsessed with the idea of finding the sharp point that
killed her baby. She finally loses all contact with reality and
wanders around in a delirium. She stumbles over a nest of
wasps, digs into it, and is stung to death. The frenzy with which
Nils and Randolv work increases after Jorunn's death until Nils
breaks under the strain. Instead of following his mother's example by shutting himself off from other people, however, he turns
to Astrid. Throughout the novel they have been slowly becoming
more and more attracted to each other, and when Nils turns to
her, Astrid responds by spontaneously accepting his need for her
and by declaring her love for him, and he is saved. Randolv
works on alone, in greater and greater frenzy, and he is on the
point of following Jorunn into insanity when he suddenly stops
at "the outermost brink"[30] when he is about to throw Nils's tools

onto the scrap pile in a desperate attempt to build it still higher. Randolv's salvation is not as definite as Nils's, but there is "a wild hope"[31] as the novel ends that he will remain sane.

The Tower is not nearly as successful a novel as its immediate predecessors. It lacks the stylistic concentration and the effective integration of images of *The Seed* and *The Bleaching Yard*. The image of the tower, split as it is between the tower of Nils's imagination and the "towering" pile of scrap, fails to focus the associations of the reader in the same way that the image of the dark barn in *The Seed* or the image of the bleaching yard does. One of the best written sections of the book is the long chapter depicting Jorunn's descent into insanity. The images employed are disturbingly evocative: when she looks out over the sound the water seems to her to be standing still, heavy and gray; as she walks across a field she thinks she sees a horse with huge eyes and its feet planted in the earth moving silently toward her; as she runs from it, she feels that there is someone walking beneath the earth with the soles of their feet pressing up against hers. There is no development, however, of the images of death which have appeared to her earlier, and of which the image of the plains, familiar from *The Sandalwood Tree,* is the most prominent. This does not diminish the feeling of horror at her condition felt by the reader, but it does lead to a sense of confusion due to the profusion of images and the failure to integrate them effectively.

The emotionally most powerful scene of the book is that in which Nils seeks and receives Astrid's love and help. It is depicted with the extreme simplicity which characterizes Vesaas' writing at its best:

"Has it become so terrible for you?"
"Yes," he answered. "I can't stand it any more."
Directly from the worries and the guilt and the rust and the entire transformed world which had formed out of it all. At the breaking-point—and she understood it, and put her arms around him. She embraced him in a way that nearly made him faint.
"Oh, Nils," she said. "I love you."[32]

This sponteaneous expression of deep concern on her part has what is essentially a shock effect on Nils, and is what makes it possible for him to step back from the brink of disaster. This scene must have been one of those which Stig Dagerman had in mind when he wrote in 1952:

Vesaas writes about people who experience insuperable difficulties. They are driven toward a spiritual destruction from which they are at last rescued, not through the agency of higher powers or external eventualities, but through the love or support or kindness of another person. The climaxes of Vesaas' books are those dazzling moments when a person steps out of himself and approaches, across a slender span of understanding, his fellow human being who is in danger.[33]

Elise Tander's desperate act of exposing both her husband's and her own shame, Karl Li's words condemning violence, Såve Dyregodt's calm advice to Klas, are all examples of other such moments in Vesaas' writing which Dagerman might have had in mind, but of all these Astrid's reaction to Nils's need for her is the one with the greatest immediate emotional impact, coming as it does in sharp contrast to the mood of hopelessness and despair built up throughout many preceding chapters.

Despite the overall lack of integration of images in *The Tower,* several of the images are of interest either in themselves or in terms of their development in later books. Bridges figure prominently in several of Vesaas' books, and usually represent a transition from a known to an unknown state. This motive appears as early as in *The Farm at Grinde,* when Toremun and Brit are standing on the threshold to adult life:

Come, the little child says, this is my country. And the adult stands at the bridge and looks across. The country of childhood is on the other side with its peaks and spires and there would be many pleasant things to meet there. Come on, the child says, and the adult wants to, but he realizes he is heavy and the span of the bridge is so fragile.

But the sun shines on the child and transforms everything. One day it is *the child* who trips over the bridge, to the world of the adult, and the bridge collapses behind it for all time.

Toremun and Brit stood at the door of a new kingdom, and the bells were ringing so beautifully over in that unknown country.[34]

This image is developed further in *The Tower:*

The woods on the other side of the sound were dark and unknown. The long bridge calmly connected it with what was known. But one's own longing was directed toward the unknown.[35]

The longing connected with the use of this motif in *The Tower* is mainly of an erotic nature. Jon is the person in the novel who is most directly involved in this, since he has a girl friend who lives "behind the ridges"[36] (which itself is a frequent image in Vesaas' writing of the unknown) on the other side of the sound, but also the relationship between Astrid and Nils develops in meetings between them beside the sound.

A second use of the bridge motif, both in *The Tower* and in Vesaas' writing in general, is to represent contact between people. This is touched on slightly in *The Tower*, but not developed at length:

> Vesla sat looking over at her parents as if from a different shore, but there was no permanent bridge over to them, as there was over the sound.[37]

A third use of the bridge motif, one developed greatly in later novels, is only hinted at in *The Tower*: the bridge as a symbol of the eternal:

> Close by, the bridge leaped out from the land, chiseled and firm, as if intended to last forever.[38]

Another important image is developed in connection with Randolv's obsession with building up the pile of scrap. Toward the end he and Nils begin dismantling automobiles with acetylene torches:

> That made it still more unearthly. It was as if the consuming flame had sprung out of something which they had held under control before, but which now had free play—and the large, dark glasses they wore disfigured them and transformed them, but perhaps showed them as they had become.[39]

The use of fire to represent a destructive, evil force is very clear here (note also that its occurrence here is connected with an image of darkness). This is a very frequent motif in Vesaas' writing from this time on. An obvious example of this, one that has already been discussed, is "The Shriek" in "Three Quiet Men," which has connections with both fire and darkness.

IV The House in Darkness

This same constellation of motifs plays a very important role in Vesaas' next novel, *The House in Darkness* (*Huset i mörkret*, 1945), which was published before both *The Bleaching Yard* and *The Tower*. It was written during the last months of the German

occupation, and reflects the mood and events of those days. It is
an allegory based on the activity of the Norwegian resistance
movement during the war, but is nevertheless remarkably universal in reference. It applies equally well to the resistance of any
democratic land to the imposition of totalitarian control. The
mood is set in the first few paragraphs:

> If someone asks what it is, this that is so large, and that is struggling
> and creaking in the darkness, then the answer is that it is a trans-
> formed house.
> It is all collected here, under one huge, billowing roof: countless
> rooms and hallways and passageways—and separated from all the
> world by a thick, heavy darkness. . . .
> The house creaks. No one really knows what it is or where it comes
> from, but there is a constant creaking. A silent storm is raging here:
> There is a tension here, which is called forth here, and which also is
> stifled to produce a creaking.[40]

The house in darkness not only creaks, it also shakes and
trembles, and the relationship to the image of the trembling dam
in the Dyregot novels is clear. The hallways of the house are lit
up only by rows of "flaming arrows," which point the way to the
center of the house. The associations of evil and destruction wakened by the images of fire and darkness are intensified by the
introduction of snake imagery. A rubber-wheeled wagon moves
along the hallways with a soft hissing sound like that of "a huge
snake."[41] This wagon comes out of the center of the house, sent
by those who live there and have power over the house, to bring
into the center those who resist that power. The overall impression the reader receives of the house in darkness is one of sup-
pression and terror.

The action of the novel centers around the work of a sabotage
group led by a young man named Stig. He is admired by a weak
collaborator who works for the oppressors by polishing the arrows in the hallways and who is known in the novel only by the
descriptive title "the arrow polisher." He is ashamed of his col-
laboration, as are also his two children, Frans and Frida. He tries
to convince himself that he must do it for his children's sake, but
he secretly dreams of being a friend of Stig and helping him in
his resistance work. He tries to strike up an acquaintance with
Stig, but is naturally snubbed, and in revenge reports Stig, who
is captured and tortured to death. The arrow polisher is then

executed by another member of the sabotage group, Peter. By means of this simple plot Vesaas has been able to illustrate many of the situations which arise under totalitarian conditions, and many of the ways in which different people react under such circumstances.

In *The House in Darkness* the tendency toward abstraction in character portrayal started in *The Seed* is more pronounced than ever before. None of the characters has more than a first name, and several are only indicated by their occupation, as for example, the arrow polisher, the minister. They represent types rather than individuals, but Vesaas has accomplished this without over-simplifying their human natures. The arrow polisher, for example, is both a complex and a moving figure. The conflict which racks him is portrayed in depth, and the reader can easily identify with him in his struggle to salvage a mite of self-esteem in the face of total humiliation.

The personal conflicts faced by the resistance workers are also discussed in depth. Not only the conflict between loyalty to family and loyalty to cause, but also the conflict between the demands of morality and the demands of their resistance activities. The sabotage group is composed of all types, from the man who feels no qualms at all at killing, to him who finds that he is unable to kill when he is called upon to do so. The moral conflict is most intense in Stig, who is responsible for the activity of the group as a whole, as well as for himself as an individual, and this responsibility weighs heavily on him. He has frequent discussions about these problems with a minister who supports the activity of the resistance movement, but fully realizes the moral conflicts involved in his position. He is also fully aware of the conflicts that will arise when the struggle is over:

"There will be something else then—but if *we* will be fit to be a part of it, that's another thing. We probably won't be. . . . It seems to me that we will be used up by what we have to take on us now. So that it will be difficult to adjust to the new conditions . . . because something *else* will be needed then, something which we can't use now. I don't know. But I become so frightened sometimes. Now sternness is needed. Later goodness will be needed, that which is and will remain through all time. It is only we who during this long night have to say and do things which cause our hearts to ache. But we have to, for those who follow us. But it is very possible that when this time is over we will be useless."[42]

This conflict is acted out within the range of the members of Stig's resistance group in the persons of Peter, who takes upon himself the responsibility of resorting to violence, and Henrik who is unable to kill when called upon to do so. They each have a vision of their role and of their limitation. Henrik wanders around, deeply ashamed of himself, after his failure to live up to his own and others' expectations of him:

But he stops again:
A sound stops him.
He feels as if something is happening inside him. And what it is is that he can apprehend such a sound. Here where it otherwise is sound-less and stifled and seemingly deserted—there is a strange sound here. Close beside the abyss itself. . . .
When he first notices it, he doesn't understand what it is, but soon he is able to comprehend it: It is the fragile but thousandfold sound of sleeping. The infinitely fragile wheezing of babies sleeping. Thou-sands and tens of thousands of them. . . .
And Henrik stands listening to it. It is somehow for him.
He is such that he can open himself to it. He has what those who are tough and stern at this moment don't have, but which must exist and must be preserved. Something related to what is revealing itself to him here. And therefore it reveals itself. . . .[43]
He tears himself away. Stumbles off. But the chorus sounds in his ears. He has been given something to hold onto, and it helps him. There will be use for him again! He will be called for. Tomorrow.[44]

Peter, on the other hand, continues working in the sabotage group, and is engaged in boring a tunnel beneath the center of the house to undermine it. He breaks through a wall and finds the bodies of those who have died in the resistance, hidden deep beneath the crushing weight of the center of the house:

He doesn't dare move. He has the feeling that it will last only as long as he is as motionless as they are. If he stretched out a finger, the walls would glide back down in front of him. Between him and them. He cannot reach them.
Up above somewhere the overloaded house creaks. But is moving in the direction of life. Peter stands there and feels: *he* will not be a part of that. His end will come *here*. In that dizzying moment he somehow becomes certain of it.[45]

It is difficult to imagine a clearer and more deep-felt statement of the moral conflicts involved in the choice between violent or nonviolent resistance to evil. Peter and Henrik each discover the course of action which is right for him, but this self-knowledge is hard won, and the responsibility it entails is heavy for both of them.

There are people living in the house who do not solve these moral conflicts in a responsible manner, but flee from them. They are represented by the stamp collector, Martin, who wishes only that others would stop making demands on him and leave him to work with his stamp collection in peace. When the demands become too insistent, and the conflicts unbearable, he withdraws completely, into a section of the house shut off from all light and sound and populated by others like him. It is clear that they are the greatest losers of all, not only in the struggle in which the house in darkness is engaged, but in the total life situation, since they have refused to commit themselves, have turned away from their responsibilities as human beings, and in this way have lost every chance to participate in life.

The problems of loyalty and interaction between members of a resistance group are also treated in the play *Morning Wind* (*Morgonvinden*) from 1947, but the presentation of these problems in this form is not as convincing as in *The House in Darkness*. In the years immediately following the end of World War II Vesaas was primarily occupied with writing poetry. His first three volumes of poems were published in 1946, 1947, and 1949, before the publication of his next novel, *The Signal* (*Signalet*, 1950). These three collections contain poems in many different styles and dealing with many different subjects. In all three there are poems which deal either directly or indirectly with experiences and impressions from the war years and with the world situation in the years immediately following the war. The one all-overshadowing fact of the postwar years is treated in these volumes of poems in varying forms, most directly in two poems in the collection *The Game and the Lightning* (*Leiken og lynet*, 1947): "Rain over Hiroshima" and "The Atomic Nucleus":

"Rain over Hiroshima"

Just as she raised her hand
to lift the teapot
there was a blinding flash—

that was all
everything was gone
they were gone
changed into steam and mist,
mysteriously, rising and mute.
A cry was not a cry in this.

But the earth in desperation raised
a clenched fist high against the heavens
in protest against mistreatment,
—against what survivors know
the world over
but cannot face:
Hiroshima—

Rising milewide veil,
they were part of it,
returned to primal matter.
A shade of steam
over a tortured world.
To be a tiny part of this.

To be part of the expanding—
But not for long.
A new phase soon followed chaos.
The veil became thick with drops,
in the eternal form of drops
without beginning or end.

They fell,
cooling, countless,
as a heavy rain
downward—

In this poem Vesaas treats not only the experience of those who
perished at Hiroshima, but also, and primarily, the experience of
those who survived, in the most inclusive sense of the word. That
everyone still living in the world is in a very real sense a survivor
of Hiroshima and bears a part of the responsibility for it, is expressed even more clearly in "The Atomic Nucleus":

The monster
we have called for
and pleaded to
has finally heard our prayers.

Are you paler?
Are you different
from how you thought you would be
—standing there at the edge of the pit?

V   The Signal

The feelings of anxiety and guilt experienced by many people
in the wake of the first atomic explosions are reflected in Vesaas'
next novel, *The Signal* (1950). The situation presented to the
reader in this novel is a shocking image of the contemporary
dilemma. The entire action takes place in a railroad station
among a group of prospective travelers and station personnel who
are waiting for the signal for departure. The signal never comes,
there is no way to find out why it never comes, there is nothing
to be done while they are waiting, and there is no hope that the
signal ever will come or that the train ever will depart. The overall atmosphere is one of futility, hopelessness, and paralysis similar to the mood of several of Samuel Beckett's plays from the
1950's.

The characters Vesaas has selected to act out this drama of
futility are types rather than individuals, and in this novel abstraction in character portrayal is carried farther than ever before.
Even the names of some of the characters are part of this extreme
stylization: Mrs. All-Paid, Mr. Power, Mr. Top, who are all pas-
sengers, and Mrs. Scrape, who cleans the cars. Others have descriptive titles: the station master, the porter, the engineer. Even
those characters with names represent types: Kristensen, the
conductor who follows the rule book to the letter and who is
"only a uniform"; Jens and Eva, a young couple in love who represent the only ray of hope in the book.

Anxiety is an important element in the feelings of these characters, they are afraid both that the signal will come and that it will
not come, but the strongest feeling they have is that of an irrational shame:

Hour of shame.
It strikes like a squall across a yard. It strikes the ever-searching
porter, the self-confident Mrs. All-Paid, the silent man who bears the
responsibility for it all, Kristensen who is only a uniform, and the dim
row of cars stretching toward the unknown locomotive—like a squall
that no one knows the origin of. The wind called Shame. The storm

called Shame. No one knows anything else. Then everything is quiet again.[46]

"The silent man who bears the responsibility for it all" is the station master, who during the entire novel stands mutely on the platform, not answering even when he is asked when the train will depart. He is in charge of everything that takes place in the station, but even he is powerless, and bears the heaviest burden of guilt and shame. He is set apart from all the others, but yet they identify with him:

They are sometimes startled, when they look at him and recognize their own features.[47]

The feeling of irrational shame which permeates *The Signal* is one of the most important motifs in Vesaas' writing in recent years. Shame as a human emotion had played a role in earlier novels, but always in circumstances where its cause was apparent. For example, the islanders in *The Seed* felt shame because of their violent behavior,[48] and Martin, the stamp collector in *The House in Darkness* is paralyzed by shame when Stig sees him about to enter the section of the house where those live who have withdrawn from the conflicts of the situation.[49] In *The Signal* the shame felt by all the characters is of a more unspecified nature, they feel a "hidden smarting,"[50] but can give no explanation of it.

Given the time of its writing it is natural to make connections between the shame felt by the characters in *The Signal* and the shame that is often felt by survivors of catastrophes.[51] That Vesaas feels that all men are survivors of Hiroshima is clear from the poem "Rain over Hiroshima"; that this feeling of shame on the part of survivors has deep roots in him is clear from his own description of his reaction to the experience of World War I:

Everything horrible from World War II hasn't been able to obliterate the memory of 1914. I was seventeen then.

Hard work was a blessing. But a clump still sat in my chest, and I felt terrible. Even if this made me into a tremendous worker, it was not because of a feeling of the joy of working, but of despair about something that could not even be identified. It was painful just to be alive.

But then I was struck by a feeling of smarting shame: the thought of all those hundreds of thousands of young people who would in those days *have* to stop living. To keep on living was certainly their only wish. And there I was complaining about my own little problems. Shame.[52]

Combined with this feeling of shame in *The Signal* is the feeling of powerlessness, and the feeling that precious time is being wasted:

A clock strikes.
Three clear, shimmering strokes, sending out rings of precious and wasted time, and then no more. . . .
Has anyone heard?
A questioning, wondering silence follows.
Even more precious time passes and is not used. It resonates, like glass under tension, and comes to nothing.[53]

For all of the characters in *The Signal* time passes and nothing is accomplished with the exception of the young couple Jens and Eva, who meet when they come to the station, fall in love, and find happiness in their dream of the journey ahead of them. But it is more than a dream, and becomes reality for them. For them the train departs, and moves through the night. They are alone together in a compartment and cannot be reached by everything that is destroying the dream for the others:

It is as if the compartment disappears. It is closed to all the forces of destruction. In the heart of the train.[54]

Eva bears a child during the long period of waiting for the train to depart, but none of the others is helped by this sign of the triumph of the creative forces of life. Only she and Jens, who have faith in life, are able to overcome their anxiety and *live* in the midst of hopelessness.

The Signal, like *The Seed* and *The Bleaching Yard,* is highly dramatic in form, and in many ways would have been more successful as a play than as a novel. This is to a great extent due to the extreme abstraction of characterization, the effect of which is somewhat forced within the framework of the novel, but if properly stylized could be very effective on the stage. The fact that the action stretches over the course of a pregnancy is only an apparent breach of the unity of time: a pregnancy is the basic unit of *life,* and the nature of life is the basic theme of *The Signal,* even though it is shown from many of its most negative sides. The central position given to the relationship between Jens and Eva, however, indicates that Vesaas' basic attitude toward the situation described in this novel is an optimistic one. The chapters dealing with their relationship were published separately, before the publication of the novel, under the title "The Dream of a Journey, ("Reisedraumen")[55] and it is precisely their ability to maintain their faith in their dream and to transform it into action that saves Jens and Eva from the hopelessness and despair that paralyze the other characters of the novel.

The importance of the dream as a counterbalance to the destructive and dehumanizing forces in life is one of the most important themes in Vesaas' writing, both prose and poetry, during the decade following the publication of *The Signal*. The final paragraph of an essay published in 1958 sums up his attitudes very well, and at the same time has particular application to the cold, mechanical atmosphere of the station and the train in *The Signal*:

We will probably just have to accept modern technology as it is. It doesn't ask our permission, in its rapid development. But we must not proceed blindly. Not even in the machine age do we have to become machines. We have a counterbalancing force within us, if we use everything we have been given. We have something that can never be installed in a machine: love and concern for our fellow human beings. We always have that with us. It is the finest thing that we have inherited and which we can pass on to others, to build up an even greater counterbalance. As long as we have that we have the prerequisites for a life in dignity, and will not have lost all control of the situation. I think we will be able to preserve our dream.[56]

CHAPTER 5

The Style and Poetry of Tarjei Vesaas

A DISCUSSION of Tarjei Vesaas' style is inseparable from a discussion of his poetry. Even his prose style is highly lyrical in nature and reflects a basically poetic attitude toward the use of language as an expressive medium. In his best works, instead of telling a story in the traditional sense he creates atmospheres and moods through the use of images and evocative language, and it is at times difficult to distinguish between prose and poetry in his books. His short stories and novels often contain passages which are in reality poems, and in his most recent books some of these passages have been set in type in such a way that they resemble poems.

This is certainly not surprising in light of the fact that much of Vesaas' earliest writing was in poetic form. It was to a great extent imitative in nature and for the most part very traditional in form (only a very few of his poems from the 1920's, for example, dispense with rhyme),[1] and very little of it is of lasting interest. In several cases some of his early poems appear in his novels and plays from the 1920's. The last stanza of a poem from 1925 appears in a slightly altered form in The Black Horses[2] and several paragraphs, set as prose, in The Farm at Grinde[3] are in reality a poem, or in the context of the story a song, complete with rhyme. The importance of the song form for the development of Vesaas' lyrical talent is underlined by the appearance of a poem in folk ballard form in the wedding scene in the play The Dwelling Places of God.[4] The poem has four four-line stanzas with a three-line refrain following each stanza. This same poem, minus the refrain lines and in a rather extensively revised form, also appears in Vesaas' first collection of poems, The Springs (1946), with the title "Folk Ballad."

I Evocative Repetition

The influence of the folk ballads of Norway on the develop-

ment of Vesaas' style appears also in his prose. The repetition
of phrases, either in the same or slightly varying form, is common in Vesaas' prose style, and produces an effect reminiscent
of that produced by the occurence of refrain lines in the ballad
form. The description of the night during which Knut Heddejor
is born (and his mother dies) in *Children of Man* is a good
example from Vesaas' earliest writing. The sentence "A night is
long," printed as a separate line, occurs three times in little
more than two pages of the description.[5] In the Dyregodt novels,
the phrase "Feel the trembling!" occurs many times, and especially in the first volume serves to add to the atmosphere of tension and anxiety generated by the dam trembling beneath the
weight of the water behind it. In *The Bleaching Yard* Old Krister
frequently repeats the words "There's so much to linen!" and
these repetitions serve to emphasize the pathetic, obsessive quality of his search for a clean shirt. The effective use of repetition
within a single prose passage is well illustrated by the description of Johan Tander's psychological state in the first pages of
the same novel (quoted in Chapter 4). The phrases "Cast [a
little] light," "too late," and the word "undertow" are each repeated three times, each group fitting within the other like a
set of Chinese boxes. The overall effect of this concentrated pattern of expression is to add to the atmosphere of extreme psychological tension being built up in the opening pages of the
novel.

The effectiveness of the evocative repetition of phrases in
poetic form can be seen in the introductory poem in Vesaas'
first collection of poetry, *The Springs*, published in 1946:

"Snow and Spruce Woods"

Home!
snow and spruce woods
mean home.

It is ours
from the very first moment.
Before anyone has said it,
that it *is* snow and spruce woods,
it has become a part of us—
and then it is always with us
forever, ever more.

> Yard-deep drifts
> around dark trees
> —that's for us!
> Part of our very being.
> Forever, ever more,
> though no one sees it,
> snow and spruce woods are a part of us.
>
> A snow-covered slope,
> and tree upon tree
> as far as the eye can reach.
> Wherever we are
> we turn toward it.
>
> And within us is a promise
> to come home.
> Come home,
> walk over to it,
> bend branches,
> —and feel with a thrill
> what it means to be where you belong.
>
> Forever, ever more
> until our inland hearts
> cease to beat.

In this poem it is not merely the fact that the phrase "forever, ever more" is repeated, but the manner in which it is repeated that makes it effective. After the initial use of the phrase, it occurs only five lines later, quickly establishing the mood of permanency which is at the heart of the poem. The final occurence of the phrase, however, is delayed while the description of the snow and the woods is developed and given deeper significance. When it does finally reappear it serves to tie all the sections of the poem together more successfully than if it had been repeated more often or at an earlier point.

Another example of evocative repetition in this poem involves the two occurrences of the word "home" in the first stanza and of the phrase "come home" in the next-to-the-last stanza. The repetition of certain key words and phrases is here the most important formal unifying feature, as it is of so many of Vesaas' poems. That he frequently employs this same technique in his prose is one of the principal causes of the blurring of the distinction between his prose style and his poetic style.

Within the phrase "forever, ever more" there is also, of course, repetition. This type of repetition, of a single word usually, in the original, not separated by a comma, is extremely common in Vesaas' writing, especially in his earliest writing, where the effect is not always fortunate. The rather indiscriminate use of this device in his writing before *The Black Horses* is one of the major causes of its highly exaggerated and sentimental flavor, but it is used more discriminately and effectively in his more mature writing, as in "Snow and Spruce Woods."

II *Elliptical Constructions*

An important and very characteristic feature of Vesaas' prose style is the use of highly elliptical sentences mentioned in connection with the quotation in Chapter 2 from the opening page of *Children of Man*. This feature, relatively infrequent in Vesaas' earliest writing, gradually developed in his writing during the 1920's and 1930's to occupy the important position it has in his mature style. A rereading of any of the passages quoted in Chapter 4 (and a great many of those quoted in Chapter 3) will supply the reader with a wealth of examples. The effect of this feature of style is to increase the sense of immediacy of the material by removing all unnecessary and distracting elements of expression. The central concept or idea of a given passage is presented to the reader in the most direct manner possible. An extreme, but good, example of this is a passage near the beginning of *The Seed*. Rolv Li sees his sister Inga walking in the woods where she often collects plants:

The bushes in front of him began quivering. A girl stepped onto the path with a couple of long green plants in her hand. She herself was tall and young.
Rolv stared at her. At this person dear to him. His sister. Inga. Seventeen.[6]

Naturally, such an extreme stylistic device must be used with caution, which Vesaas generally does. The effect is enhanced, and held under control, by juxtaposing such highly elliptical sentences with sets of normal sentences, as in the above example. Even though the use of such elliptic constructions is not unknown in the prose style of other Norwegian writers, it is quite rare. There are few examples in nineteenth-century Scandinavian literature which might have served Vesaas as a model for the development of this feature of style, and it seems most reasonable to assume that its extreme frequency in his writing is more a result of his natural tendency toward brevity and directness of expression, whether it be oral or written, than any conscious effort to develop or establish a literary pattern. It is worth noting, however, that Vesaas' use of elliptical sentences is often reminiscent of the style used in stage directions, and this can be seen to be connected with the great emphasis on dramatic form that is apparent in his novels, and especially those written after 1940.

III   *The Impersonal Pronoun*

Another stylistic feature which occurs with high frequency in Vesaas' writing is his peculiar use of the third person singular impersonal pronoun, *one*. At its most effective, his employment of this pronoun expands a specific situation into one with universal application. A clear and obvious example is the passage in *The Seed* quoted in Chapter 4 in which the human personality is depicted as a landscape, the second paragraph of which, if translated literally, would read: "One sees oneself, and sees within oneself, etc." The pronoun when used here refers most immediately to the characters in the novel who have just taken brutal revenge on the murderer and have been forced to look at themselves, but it is also broad enough in its reference to include the author and the reader. It has similarly universal application in the passage in *The Unknown Men* in which Klas begins to be aware of the problem of responsibility: "Something began rising up on the horizon, something called responsibility. How is one supposed to bear *that?*"

Vesaas' use of this pronoun in this particular manner developed gradually, as did his use of elliptical constructions, in the course of his writing career. It is relatively rare in his earliest books in the 1920's, but he employed it with increasing frequency and skill in his writing in the 1930's. At first its use can be a bit exaggerated (for example, from *Father's Journey*: "One was past New Year's now."[7]) or hesitant and inconsistent (for example, from *Sigrid Stallbrokk*: "He didn't take cover; one felt today like tramping through wet moss and soil, and getting soaked."[8]), but it was soon brought under control. In *The Sandalwood Tree* the mother frequently uses it in her speech:

"One is alone, Magnus."
"Yes, you often say that," he answered brusquely.
"Yes, but one never feels as alone as now—."[9]

This bit of dialogue immediately precedes the passage quoted in Chapter 3 which describes the death of the mother. The extreme loneliness she feels is that of the individual facing death, the ultimate situation in which one *is* only *one,* and thus the use of this pronoun here is natural, though still unusual.

Vesaas' use of this pronoun is also often very personal, in the sense that he uses it to express his own feelings through the medium of a character. It is used in this way, for example, in a scene from *The Great Cycle* in which Per feels great loneliness even though he is surrounded by people at a Christmas party:

She said it in a sort of impoverished way. Her eyes reflected something one felt in oneself. One was alone. One was like a frightened animal, that's what one was. Look, over there on the benches the grown-ups were sitting stiffly and staring at the tree like children. One belonged nowhere.[10]

Vesaas also makes frequent use of the impersonal pronoun in this manner in his autobiographical writing, especially when he is directly discussing his own feelings (see, for example, the quotations in Chapters 3 and 4, where he is discussing his feelings toward war). It thus also seems to be a natural manner of expression for him, which he uses when he wishes to hold what he is talking about off at a distance, and which he has employed in his writing and developed into a strikingly effective literary device.

IV   The Early Poems

A good example of Vesaas' use of this feature of style in his poetry is to be found in the last two lines of the next-to-last verse of "Snow and Spruce Woods" (which, if translated literally, would read: "—and feel so that a shock runs through one/ what it means to be where one belongs"). This is, of course, a highly universal usage of this pronoun, but also here the personal implications are very strong. Several of the poems in Vesaas' first collection of poetry, *The Springs,* are quite personal in tone. The autobiographical poem "An Evening in Verona" has already been quoted in Chapter 3 and discussed there. Two poems, "Snow in a Face" and "The Boy on the Stone," are sensitive evocations of adolescent erotic fantasies and both are closely connected with episodes described in prose form in *The Great Cycle*.

It is easy to draw connections between quite a few of the poems in this collection and Vesaas' prose writing of the 1920's and 1930's. The poem "Linen," for example, stands in a very close relationship to the scenes in *The Black Horses* where Lisle takes refuge from her conflicts in the handling of her linens, and "The Woman in the Aspen Grove" describes the situation of an old farm woman near the end of her days who is strongly reminiscent of Per Bufast's mother in *The Women Call: Come Home*. The words used to describe Per's mother, and also Kari Ness in *The Seed*, occur again: tall and thin and dark-clad, but none of the somber aspects of the situation makes its appearance here. The overall tone is one of calm and contentment such as Per experiences in his old age at the end of *The Women Call: Come Home*.

Many of the poems in this first collection are thus expressions in a different form (all in rhymed verse except "Snow and Spruce Woods" and two shorter poems) of situations occurring in Vesaas' prose writing of the 1920's and 1930's, or of different aspects of those situations. As in the case of his prose writing at that time, these attempts to express himself in traditional lyrical forms were not always as successful as his later work, when he had freed himself of the restraints of regular, rhymed verse. Typically for Vesaas, the impulses that led to this change came from foreign influences. As early as 1931 he became seriously interested in modern verse form, to which he was introduced by the poetess who was to become his wife, Halldis Moren. She gave him a collection of the poetry of the Finnish-Swedish poetess Edith Södergran, and this led eventually to a radical change in his attitudes toward lyric form.[11] It was many years before the effects of this influence manifested themselves, however, and the free verse form was not dominant in his poetry until his second collection, *The Game and the Lightning* (1947).

In *The Game and the Lightning* and the three collections of poetry and various separately published poems which have followed, he has not totally dispensed with traditional form, however, and occasional poems in rhymed verse make their appearance. An entire group of seven poems in the collection *The Land of Hidden Fires* (*Löynde eldars land*, 1953), for example, are in rhymed verse of various types. It is characteristic that all of these are descriptions of scenes or portraits of people of Vesaas' native Telemark, and are similar in tone and form, though more concentrated and convincing in execution, to many of the poems in *The Springs*.

V   Themes and Imagery in the Later Poems

As in the case of *The Springs*, a number of poems in his later collections are direct expressions in poetic form of situations or atmospheres in his prose writing. The poem "Clean Dress" from *The Land of Hidden Fires*, for example, reflects the mood of *The Bleaching Yard* ("Smell the fragrance:/All dirt washed away,/the linen remains") and the poem "Along the Tracks" from the same collection reflects several scenes in *The Signal*. The title of the poem "The Wandering Tower" from the collection *The Happiness of Travelers* (*Lykka for ferdesmenn*, 1949) is identical with the title of a chapter in *The Tower* and presents in concentrated form the image of the tower as a symbol of conscience described in several of the chapters in that novel.

In most cases, however, the relationship between the poems in Vesaas' last four collections and his prose writing is less direct, and restricts itself to a natural similarity of themes and images. The question of the responsibility of the individual, which is so central to the Dyregodt novels and *The Seed*, for example, is the theme of many of the poems in these collections. Some of the most prominent images of these novels appear in connection with this theme in the poem "Responsibility" from *The Game and the Lightning*:

> Clearly,
> as on a luminous winter night
> you understand what the human spirit is.
>
> You cool your feverish brow
> against the iciness of the windowpane
> at this late hour,

anxiously
because there are no longer any boundaries
and *you* and *space* become one
and you are there bearing the entire burden
and there would be an avalanche, a storm
and disaster
if you forgot that.
Drops of sweat form
on your brow
at the thought
of your responsibility.
And when you cool your brow
at the window
you see a flash of fire outside:
flaming eyes
come back from the jungle.
lying in wait.

Weary
you cool your brow
and prepare for battle.

Fire imagery in connection with the theme of responsibility is also prominent in the poem "Inscriptions" from *The Land of Hidden Fires*:

Those inscriptions shine brightest
which are written in fire:
The truth of the brotherhood of man
is shining brightly—
The lie about the glory of war is viciously exposed.
The message of each man's responsibility
is also written in flames.

Those inscriptions shine brightest
in the atomic age
—which is the fruit of violence through thousands of years.
Our thousands of small unfriendly deeds.
We have all matured a tiny nucleus of death.

Those inscriptions shine brightest
which we refuse to see.
We read them in the dark
when we should be sleeping.

This poem which, in similarity with "The Atomic Nucleus"

(quoted in Chapter 4), discusses directly the responsibility of the individual for the present world political situation, also touches on the plight of those who attempt to avoid their responsibility. This theme, treated in prose form in the person of Martin in *The House in Darkness,* occupies an even more prominent position in the poem "The Storm Is Raging Far Above" in the collection *The Game and the Lightning*:

> The storm is raging far above.
> Noses pressed against the grass,
> to escape it.
>
> The storm's costly day—
> A long journey calls us:
> come. Join in.
>
> We lie among withered straws of grass.
> We lie among shredded hopes.
> Far above, the good we have dreamed of passes by.
>
> Frightened eyes
> that blink at lightning
> will never see a flaming tree.
>
> We doze off
> and know this all too well.
> We dig in still deeper.
>
> The storm is raging far above,
> transforming, fulfilling,
> raging past.

In this case, it is the entire life situation which is presenting the challenge for the individual to make a commitment, not just a war situation, but the conclusion is the same as in *The House in Darkness*: the result of a refusal to commit oneself is the loss of the opportunity to take part in life. The portraying of life as "a long journey" and "the good we have dreamed of" connects the imagery of this poem with that of the novel *The Signal* as well. This is a good example of the way in which Vesaas, in his poetry, frequently links together themes and images treated separately in different prose works. The imagery in his poetry, where it is generally not constrained by the necessity of conforming to the development of a plot, is also often more complex than in prose works with related themes. This is true, for example, of the fire imagery in "Inscriptions" and "The Storm Is Raging Far Above." In the novels of the war and immediate postwar period, fire is generally employed to represent a negative, destructive force. In "Inscriptions," however, it clearly represents a positive force, while in "The Storm Is Raging Far Above" it is both a destructive force, coming as a bolt of lightning, and an inspiring, positive force, appearing as a flaming tree. This dual usage of fire imagery is frequent in Vesaas' more recent writing, both prose and poetry, where it is employed to represent a force within man which can find either positive or negative, constructive or destructive expression. That this force is a hidden, latent one is clear from the title of the poetry collection *The Land of Hidden Fires*, and the poem "The Surface Is Calm" in this collection presents the image clearly and concisely:

> The surface is calm
> in the land of fires,
> nothing can be seen,
> everything is in balance.
>
> But things are happening
> in this hour,
> like flaming avalanches
> in inner mountains.
> They know it, those few
> who have seen through the fissures
> and felt the heat below.
>
> People are drawn to people
> by a hunger for fire across thousands of miles
> —and suddenly are no longer uncertain,
> eye to eye
> and with each other, about the truth about
> the fire's depth and the fire's wild meeting.

The "flaming avalanches/in inner mountains" of this poem are reminiscent of the description of the "inner landscape" in *The Seed*. The portrayal of the human personality and the course of human life in terms of landscape imagery is found in many of Vesaas' poems, and water imagery is particularly frequent in this connection. This is not surprising in light of the significance which he himself attaches to the image-forming powers of the movement of water through the landscape: "All my life

watercourses have been a stimulation for my imagination. Flowing water. The unbelievable network."[12]

The image of the movement of water through the landscape is
used to express the constantly changing course of life in the
poem "Between Breaths" in *The Land of Hidden Fires,* where
life is seen as a journey.

> ... through narrow sounds.
> ... both where the ridges above
> are dark and the bottoms depthless,
> as well as where the water is shallow
> and covered with yellow sand
> and where there are thousands of tiny islands
> and a little lake wanders happily among them.
>
> May everything that is you
> be always with you, feeling,
> before it is too late:
> There is a pulling from the mouth of the river.
> The current is stretched out in the water
> like billowing hair.

The presence of a pulling or sucking force, a natural part of
water imagery, is central to several of Vesaas' finest poems. In
the poem "Rowing" from *The Happiness of Travelers* it is a
force to be resisted:

> The day is over
> —and there is the sound of rowing.
> The dark cliff,
> darker than the evening,
> leans out over the water
> with its black creases:
> A distorted face
> with its mouth submerged.
> No one knows everything.
>
> The sound of rowing
> in circles,
> because the cliff is pulling.
> Bewildered splashing on the deep.
> Exhausted creaking of wood.
> Bewildered faithful soul who is rowing
> and can soon be pulled under. ...

Such a sucking force does not appear only in connection with water in Vesaas' poetry, nor is it always a force to be resisted. In the poem "Tired Tree," also in *The Happiness of Travelers,* it appears as a natural and inevitable part of life:

> In a valley
> which no one frequents
> the largest tree
> has fallen,
> spread wide,
> with twigs and branches
> pressed against the earth
> as if in an embrace
> after endless longing.
>
> Thrown itself down,
> and the reasons are obscure,
> for there has been no storm.
> But there it lies
> as if at a goal.
>
> There it lies blind and deaf,
> and wants but one thing,
> and gets it
> —for the grass has already begun
> the quiet, gripping drama
> that will take place.
> The grass has already begun growing
> in between the branches.
> It will grow long in the shelter there,
> and wither and fall back like faded hair
> by autumn,
> and next year it will grow up again
> longer, and cover more,
> and mold and moss will start
> their hidden sucking,
> and the grass will grow up and fall down
> and grow up and fall down
>
> as the years go by
> and mold and moss consume,
> and the tree will lie unmoving
> deeper and deeper in its embrace
> and begin to be *the other*—
> while the grass grows and falls back

like pale, familiar hair
—and everything is long since gone
and a hundred years is as a
moment
for that which lasts.

In this poem the emphasis is placed on the final stages of existence. The relationship to the basic theme of the interrelationship of the life and death processes of the Bufast novels and *The Sandalwood Tree* is obvious, but the poem has greater universal application.

Tree imagery also appears in Vesaas' poems in connection with the creative forces of life. In a charming little poem entitled "Once Upon a Time" in *The Game and the Lightning* the awakening sexual feelings of a young girl are likened to the coming of spring to a tree:

There was a little birch
which had been promised new leaves
in the middle of May.
She hardly touched the ground
because of it
and because she was so slight.

And it came as promised, too,
a May wind.
He made her giddy
and sweet in the bark
and sore in all her buds.
A bird came and settled
on a naked branch
and said the time had come—

She felt nothing
all day long.
But when evening had come
her nakedness and slightness
were tinged with green.
Strange and transformed.

Giddy and alive.
She released herself, slowly.
Freed herself of her roots, she thought.
Sailed like a pale green veil over the ridge.
Away from there forever,
—thought the little birch.

In the poem "You and I Alone in Silence" in *The Game and the Lightning* the imagery of water and trees is combined to create an atmosphere of mystery around the situation of two people seeking, and finding, each other:

> Like an evening's rain
> after a scorching day—
>
> The parched ferns
> are slowly called back to life
> by what is happening now.
>
> Heaven and earth—
> what is one and what the other?
> One is filled with the other
> at such a time,
> by this flow of sweet.
>
> A fragrance one never learned of
> in all the years of learning
> —now it is here
> beside my cheek.
>
> And while the wet dusk deepens
> the paths on the water blur,
> as if to be walked on when all is over,
> and the trees on the shore are not trees
> but you and I alone in the silence
> and the shore is no longer any shore
> or boundary.

The importance of contact, not only between people or between people and nature, but also between people and animals is a very important motif running through all of Vesaas' writing. In Vesaas' prose works the animal standing in the closest relationship to man is the horse, but in his poetry birds are more prominent in this respect, although the horse does appear occasionally in this role (cf., for example, the final lines of the poem "The Field" in *The Game and the Lightning*: "But we saw a white horse wading through the grass alone,/ and we recovered a shining dream from our childhood.") The poem "The Loons Fly North" in *The Game and the Lightning* evokes beautifully the significance that can be attached to the sight of birds:

High as specks against the clouds,
alone although they are two,
the loons fly north,
and disappear.

A single chilling hoot
reaches us
standing below
in great confusion.

Once out of sight
they plummet down
toward an icy lake
which has stirred a secret warmth.

We like to hear such things—
a lonely wild heart
reaching down to us
out of its boundless freedom.

In his most recent collection of poetry, *May Our Dream Stay New* (*Ver ny, vår draum,* 1956), Vesaas assigns still deeper significance to this image. The final poem in the collection, "May Our Dream Live," a long poem in three sections, opens:

Live,
our dream.
Stay always new.

The bird in the distant clouds.
High high
—and you will never come down to us,
because we,
far below,
have sent you up.

The importance for Vesaas of the dream, and its significance for those who hope to participate fully in life, has already been discussed in connection with the novel *The Signal.* This important theme is also present in the poem "The Storm is Raging Far Above" (quoted above), which was written before *The Signal,* and it appears frequently in other poems written during the 1940's and 1950's. It finds its most effective and lyrical expression, however, in the image of the bird in the distant clouds in "May Our Dream Live." The dream, distant and unattainable as it is, is nevertheless indispensable to man, and the poem ends:

> Stay new,
> you bear our name,
> and our features.
> You bear our life
> forever.

CHAPTER 6

Lyrical Realism: Short Stories and Novels 1952-1959

I Short Stories

AFTER the publication of the volume of short stories *The Clay and the Wheel* in 1936, eighteen years were to pass before Vesaas published his next collection of short stories, *The Winds* (*Vindane*, 1952). During the 1940's he devoted most of his time and creative energy to the writing of novels and poems, but his production of short stories never ceased completely. A number of the stories included in *The Winds* were written during those years, and several were published either during or shortly after the war. Two of these, "Grain Across the Sea," first published in 1942,[1] and "Naked," first published in 1946,[2] are directly concerned with problems arising from the war. Some words from an essay written in 1939 sum up Vesaas' attitudes toward life and the situation at that time and provide a basis for understanding the imagery in these stories, as well as in the novel *The Seed*:

> The sun and the seasons cannot be touched by dictatorship, and man is helpless before this great drama of nature. The foundations of life stream out of an eternal sun, and in company with it are the great events of human life: birth, love, death, rebirth.[3]

Further background for the story "Grain Across the Sea" is provided by two stories from *The Clay and the Wheel*, "Twenty-one" (discussed in Chapter 3) and "Bread." In "Twenty-one" the young couple meet and fall in love during the grain harvest, and the sun and its effect are central in the story:

> Father placed the grain on the poles. Turned the sheaves toward the sun like a golden stream. The sun streamed down in return.[4]

And when the couple meet in the evening after the day's work in the grain field it is beside a large stone:

It was a good place. The large stone calmly radiated the warmth of the sun it had been absorbing all day long.[5]

"Bread" is a story about the grain harvest itself, about the effect it has on the lives of those, both young and old, working in it, and about the "awe at watching *the bread* ripen out in the fields."[6] It describes with great intensity the mood of expectation one hot, sunny day just before the beginning of the grain harvest, and by emphasizing the ritualistic aspects of the harvest it shows how the work consecrates not only the basic food which results from it, but also the lives of those engaged in it. Both these stories are paeans to the elemental life forces and to the source of energy, the sun, behind them.

In "Grain Across the Sea" the chain of events which leads from the grain ripening in the fields to the bread in the mouths of hungry people has been disrupted:

It is different now. Wartime.

The demands are more urgent. Because the sea lanes are closed.

The miller has lately begun thinking about *the mountain*—until a mill has started grinding inside his brain, too. He can't rid himself of it; it rumbles like something that will soon burst out in flame. There are mountains of grain in the world! *Now.* But not here.[7]

It is not only the blocking of the shipping lanes that has disrupted the progression of the grain from raw material to food, but also the condition of the miller who is the central figure in the story. He is on the point of breaking under the strain of both overwork and the thought of all those who do not have enough to eat throughout the world. He begins, in the shadowy light of the mill at night, to see apparitions: emaciated men scraping flour dust off the walls and searching for single grains on the floor and in the empty sacks. But he feels that he must hold his peace and bear up under the strain:

He has a feeling that if he lets it slip a horrible avalanche will sweep over the world. His silence is the last thing restraining it. That is holding things in place.[8]

The beneficial heat of the sun which had ripened the grain has been replaced in the story by what is, for the miller, the killing heat of the drying room, where he is working. The mill trembles in the darkness as the grindstones turn, and it finally seems to the miller that the roof is about to collapse:

There is no more resistance in him, so his legs begin to sag. Not the mill, but he himself collapses in the dark. He only wishes fervently that something incomprehensible would somehow happen so that this mountain would start moving and come across.
Come across—
It is for us, too—[9]

But as in both *The Seed* and *The House in Darkness*, there is something within man which allows him to retain faith in life and the future. When the miller recovers his senses the sound of the grindstones no longer represents a threat of destruction to him, but rather a sign of hope:

And at the same time something fills him. A helping hand he has won for himself. A feeling of certainty builds up within him: the mountain off in the distance *is* moving!
It will come. . . .
The grindstones rumble. But there is no one scraping flour off the walls. The weakness has left the miller. He believes that the mountain will come. The grain is streaming here as always, and it is streaming everywhere. Flowing between the grindstones toward its consummation. On its stirring journey toward people.[10]

The motif of the constancy of the life energy which ultimately comes from the sun, which is central to these short stories and *The Seed*, finds its most poignant expression in the three-page story "Naked." It begins:

She has left behind a nameless child here—in a violated, silent land.
There probably has never been anyone as alone as this child. He has simply arrived, and is lying there in the open. The day spreads out its clearness above him, and he reaches for it, thinking that there is something for him in all this.
No one bends down to him and asks what his name is. He has probably not been given any name. Nothing quite so naked has ever come from the womb.
He moves his wax-white finger through the air in the form of a bow. It is just a tiny movement down at the bottom of something that concerns no one.[11]

The child's father is a German soldier stationed in Norway during the war, and its mother a Norwegian girl whose family has turned against her because of the shame. This background is suggested in a few short paragraphs, but the main attention in the story is focused on the abandoned baby. It lies there in the open, feeling the wind and the stones and the straws around it, and is receptive to it all, "waiting for what he doesn't know."[12] The fog and the cold and the darkness of the night which come make him whimper, but he lives on, and in the final paragraph Vesaas develops still further the image of the bow, an image he employs frequently to represent the transition state between life and death:

He is alive. The sun is flaming somewhere, and is for everyone. It will appear again, with renewed blinding light. He didn't die during this night either. He is lying on his back, waiting for something that he knows absolutely nothing about. He is nameless seven times over, but he is waiting nevertheless. His feeble finger makes a feeble motion. A tiny bow against the huge vault of space—but it was from east to west all the same.[13]

The image of the sun as a renewing force is also employed in the opening paragraph of another of the stories in *The Winds* which was originally published shortly after the war, "The Little Tike,"[14] but the tone in this story is much lighter, and it is one of Vesaas' most charming children's portraits:

His eyes are barely above the top of the desk, like a tiny sun above a mountain ridge. But there is nothing about them reminiscent of evening—he radiates a spirit of rising, becoming, of an expectation of development.[15]

The little boy is waiting to get a chance to recite his lesson for the school board which is monitoring the class of a new, young teacher. Things are not going well, and she becomes more and more nervous. She knows that her youngest pupil knows his lesson, and will make a good impression on the board, but she hesitates to call on him:

She is new and inexperienced, and needs something to lean on. She realizes that the only thing she can completely depend on is Little Tike, and she doesn't dare use it up. If she were to start him off, he would run empty in a moment, and she would be worse off than ever. Sitting there, he is at least a promise of something.[16]

His sheer enthusiasm and rapt attention serve as a constant inspiration and help to her, and enable her to get through the hour safely. His chance to recite finally comes, and he launches into the lesson he knows so well:

The time has come. And he hasn't forgotten a bit of what he has learned. It's all ready to come pouring out, just like a bag of peas. But he is so excited by it all that the words don't sound! . . . He is like a mute telling about great happenings, and his words are only warm air. But he knows it so well! He doesn't realize that he is making no sound; he is happy and excited and puffs the lesson out of his mouth.[17]

Such portraits of children as this one of Little Tike give the impression of being more descriptions of their world as seen from within than the result of observation of them from without. This must undoubtedly be seen in connection with Vesaas' apparent ability to perceive and react to life in the way in which children do, as discussed in Chapter 1. One of the best descriptions of the way in which a child reacts to a situation is to be found in the story "The Gingerbread Man" in *The Winds*. It is a four-page description of the impatience of a little girl on Christmas Eve. She can hardly contain her excitement at the thought of all the presents, and is most fascinated by the gingerbread man on the Christmas tree which she catches sight of during a stolen peek into the living room:

It was all so strange. It was almost unbearable. It was all for her; she knew that well enough, but it didn't help just knowing it—you could *never* know. As she stood there at that moment, during the last few exciting minutes of waiting, it was as if it had never happened before and had never been told about before. Almost unbearable. Her world was a thousand miles high and a thousand miles deep—she didn't understand the least bit about it, but understood all the same, and now she was standing there in the doorway and her throat was dry.[18]

There are many such sympathetic descriptions of the child's view of the world in Vesaas' short stories, from that of the two little boys who try to reach heaven by climbing up a ladder toward the patch of blue sky they see at its top in the story "When There Was a Path to Heaven" in his first collection, *The Bell in the Knoll* from 1929, to the four little children who venture into the woods in search of a moose in the story "The Adventure" in his last collection, *One Fine Day* (*Ein vakker dag*, 1959). They are playing and quarreling together, and trying to find something to do to pass the time:

It was Sunday and they were wandering around looking for something worth seeing or hearing. Anything was welcome on a long Sunday afternoon.[19]

They are walking through the woods talking about everything strange there is to be found there. One of them mentions the moose, and a mood of awe falls over them:

Ah, the moose. It had been called forth—that which they had never seen, but which was there all the same. The moose was there. Someone had seen it once on a nearby mountainside. It was everything that was looming and hidden that they thought of but did not talk about.[20]

They meet an old man who has been sitting in the sun at the edge of the woods and thinking about the days of strength and vitality that are forever past for him. They tell him that they are going to look for the moose, and ask him to join them. He is caught up in their enthusiasm:

The old man stood in the waves flowing from them, and they were not ordinary waves. He began tingling and pulsing all over, gripped by something which had nearly been forgotten in his period of great decline: strength and splendor. The moose in the woods. A call from something he had had to leave. The children stood around him and bound him to them.[21]

They all set off, and they actually do see the moose suddenly go storming past them through the woods:

What now happened was over in a flash, and for the rest of their lives was surrounded by an aura of wildness and enchantment and hearts in throats—and a wonderful giddiness when it was all over and they were safe. But this applied only to the four children, who had room for all things. It was different for the old man who stood in their midst and had to bear the brunt of the meeting, and who was stiff and brittle....

He saw what was coming as renewal, in the strong, golden light filtering through the leaves, as if it were a messenger from the sun. Surrounded by a blinding light came everything which had once been his: strength, vitality, adventure, all the odors of youth and manhood—it stormed toward him, and the four children who were clutching him from all sides sent their own excitement coursing fourfold through his channels, which were not able to expand to accept it all. They *had* to burst.

They split along old cracks and collapsed. Gone, but in a flaming blaze. Finished for good. A stripe across the path of the four little children.

They were clutching the old man so tightly that they were pulled along by his fall into the underbrush as the moose stormed past.[22]

In this story Vesaas has succeeded in presenting in a single image the demands life makes on people, whether they be young or old. The moose represents both the glories in life that are past for the old man and all that life has in store for the children. The children have unlimited ability to receive the onrush of life, but the old man's system can no longer open itself to the infinitude of possibilities that there are in life. The ultimate source of strength and vitality in this story is once again the sun, but its agent here is the large untamed animal whose presence is both tempting and threatening. This motif makes its appearance in two earlier short stories, "Glorius the Bull" in *The Clay and the Wheel* and "The Wild Horseman" in *The Winds*. "Glorius the Bull" is a story about unbridled pride and arrogance in which the strength and potency of the bull is relished vicariously by its owner, with calamitous results, while "The Wild Horseman" deals with more elusive feelings. In *The Sandalwood Tree* Vesaas had described the difficulties that the father frequently had in writing under the pressure of the necessity of earning money for food and lodging. In "The Wild Horseman" the problem is discussed in greater detail. An author finds that his creative powers have dried up under the pressure of the thought of his responsibilities as a provider for his small son. The conflict he feels is intensified when it becomes apparent that his son is very ill. During a trip to the city where the boy is to be operated on they see a bull run rampant:

The powerless father drank deeply of the sight. Such bursting energy. Blood thick and red and pulsating through its veins. He looked at it thirstily.[23]

This episode, which was originally published separately (in a slightly different form) in 1946 with the title "Power,"[24] is central to the story both in terms of its location and its idea content. As in the case of the moose in "The Adventure," the bull represents different things to the father and the son. The little boy is both frightened and fascinated by the sight, and the reader is given a forewarning of his fate in a scene which follows the killing of the bull:

The bus roars and drives slowly past the café. They pass a wall of bushes. Svein is sitting beside the window looking out. His father is sitting beside him. What's that! They both start violently. They see something, just a glimpse as the bus gathers speed:

From beneath the lush leaves the large dark head of a dog protrudes, its mouth full of the warm innards of the bull. The dog's gaping mouth and its intense eyes lend the scene a shocking, unearthly quality.[25]

The operation is unsuccessful, and Svein dies, but this is not an unalloyed tragedy for the father. At the moment of the child's death, as he looks into his dying son's eyes, at the light shining there, he feels his creative powers returning to him:

"What sort of man am I," he thinks, shocked.
Shame.
But it was no use. It swelled up within him of its own accord.
I mustn't lose any of this. . . .
I'll write a story the likes of which I've never written before. About the light that I saw! I'm saved, he thinks, blushing with shame.[26]

In addition to these stories, in which Vesaas makes use of animals to represent various aspects of human life, he has also written several excellent stories in which the situations of the animals themselves are the focus of the story. In the story "Japp" in *One Fine Day* the panic of a dog whose master has fallen off a cliff and left it clinging to a narrow mountain ledge is chillingly described, and in "The Horse from Hogget" in the same collection Vesaas depicts with great skill the quiet desperation of a horse that has fallen through the ice of a marsh in the mountains. The desperation felt by the two young boys who are with the horse is as great as his:

[The horse] looked at them. Moved his muzzle back and forth across the surface of the dirty water and kept his nostrils just barely clear.
Don't scream, whatever you do.
He moved his muzzle back and forth, whatever he did that for. But he kept silent.[27]

The boys work feverishly to get the horse out of the marsh, and after several hours of work finally succeed. They are close to the farm's reserve haybarn in the mountains, and lead the horse to it

with its hidden summer in the darkness. It was almost unbelievable.

They got the door open, and luckily it was high enough so that the horse could get in. There was hay. But not full. There was room for all. But dark.

Come come.

He understood them. Walked right into the fragrant summer.[28]

They work feverishly to warm the horse and cover him, and the lyrical description of the life-giving qualities of the hay dispels the last traces of the mood of desperation and terror built up earlier:

They could barely manage to contain the torrent within them. Oh, we are brushing you and rubbing you, and brushing you and rubbing you! and packing round you all the herbs which make the mountains fragrant—that's it! Everything that grows on green slopes and is full of spices and is good throughout eternity—[29]

Two of Vesaas' most fascinating stories about animals are "A Daring Ant" in *The Winds*[30] and "In the Fish's Golden Youth" in *One Fine Day*. The point of view in each of these stories is that of the creature of the title, but it is at the same time not difficult to see them as representations of human types. The ant is cantankerous and aggressive:

He was dry and lean and daring. Ready to face anything which might be in his way. Everything was an enemy. He tasted the air. In the ant hill the air was sharp and bitter—out here in the grass it was much too mild. Kid stuff. It really irritated him. In addition, he got his feet wet from the dew which hadn't dried completely yet. But he pushed on.[31]

He atttacks everything that he comes across: other ants, worms, a snail. He eats bugs he runs across, but they don't taste like anything, and the worse they taste the angrier he becomes, and the angrier he becomes the worse they taste. A cow happens to be in his path, but the ant doesn't hesitate:

The ant went right over and began biting into it, but couldn't rip anything loose. Anger boiled inside him. Suddenly the cow turned over on its side and lay down on top of him. He struggled and thrashed about. Squashed. Thrashed about and burrowed ahead between the flattened blades of grass. The cow's full stomach rumbled above him like a violent thunderstorm.

Finally he came out into the open again. He wasn't as squashed as he had thought. But he certainly wasn't all smiles. He bit furiously into the cow and pulled as hard as he could. The cow didn't budge. He emptied his acid tank into her. Then he left.[32]

But the world finally proves to be too much even for the daring ant. He scrambles into a house and into a bowl of sugar:

A little later the piece of sugar was lifted out of the bowl and dropped into a cup of boiling-hot coffee. The sugar melted out of his stiffened claws and he floated to the top. He had come to the end of the line.
He was quickly splashed out through the open window, together with the other contents of the cup. A whistling bow out over the grass. Small specks came up out of the earth and began to eat him.[33]

"In the Fish's Golden Youth" is also a story about the dangers awaiting the unwary along the path of life, but the fish is more innocent and of a milder nature than the ant:

He was a trout in a stream. A he-fish weighing just a quarter of a pound. But he was really a fine little trout, with olive green and silver stripes along his sleek body, and purple dots right where they suited him best.
The stream he lived in ran into a large pool here—actually it was more of a lake than a pool—with the bottom somewhere far down in the murky depths. Unknown. Many giants loomed out of the Black Deep and sank back down again. Their presence was a fearful mystery.[34]

The little fish is both frightened and fascinated by the mysteries of the depths of the pool. He watches as large fish eat smaller ones, and as fish are pulled out of the water in nets or on hooks. All of this gives him much to think about, and he likes to lie lazily in the current with his snout against "a special thinking-stone he had."[35] He is bewildered by everything he sees around him, but it doesn't occur to him to be dismayed; he merely keeps growing, and playing the role that is his:

He didn't think for a second: and me just a little fish. With a few sharp flicks of his growing tail he overtook and gobbled down the first one he saw of his own size. It all happened by itself and had no meaning whatsoever.[36]

The relationship of the little fish, and everything around him in his pool, to the overall pattern of existence of which he is only a tiny part is made clear by the final image of the story:

At this moment a jolt went through all the water whether it was flowing or still, down to the unknown depths—like the striking of a mute bell, even though there was nothing of the sort. A jolt could definitely be felt, however. It was the sun which had risen over the water and over all life.

The sun greeted all its living things, warm and cold—but it was nevertheless too far away and too large, unaware of how things really were. It was as if in passing it said something much too simple to them, with its carefree beaming smile.[37]

Vesaas has also written directly about the apprehensions and hesitancies of youth in a number of short stories. Three of these in his first two collections, "Signe Tone," "Twenty-one," and "Nils Fet," were discussed in Chapter 3, and "Last Man Home" in *The Winds* served as the basis for much of the discussion in Chapter 1. All of these stories deal, in one way or another, with the manner in which young people adjust to the demands which approaching adulthood makes of them. The two longest stories in *One Fine Day*, "Blue Button Lost" and "Mist Rain," are among Vesaas' finest studies of the problems and conflicts that accompany the process of growing to sexual maturity. In "Mist Rain" Vesaas uses the same image to convey the mood of sexual expectancy as in "Signe Tone": the light mist rain which "*is* just something, sort of. Something that settles on you," as one of the girls in the story expresses it.[38] The story deals with the complexities of the relationships between three girls and three boys, all of them seventeen to eighteen years old: a tangled web of hopes and jealousies and infatuations, but also, perhaps the hesitant beginnings of lasting love.

The six teen-agers are all at a dance, and spend the evening wandering in and out of the dance hall, and through the neighboring woods. Their conversations are full of clumsy expressions of their confused feelings, small sudden outbursts and pregnant pauses. That there is such a high percentage of dialogue in this story is due to the fact that it was originally written as a radio play, in which form it was even more successful as an evocation of the mood of hesitancy and expectancy of young love than as a short story. The sounds of approaching steps on gravel, the jangling of a bicycle bell, the singing of birds as the full light of day begins to return, and the sensitive reading of the lines in the fine production by the Norwegian Broadcasting Service in 1958 provided many nuances which words on a page cannot communicate, no matter how skillfully they are put together. The radio play is an art form which suits Vesaas' purposes extremely well, and he produced some of his finest work in this form. He has himself explained why this is so in an article entitled "Remote-control Theater":

> In listening to a radio play the listener must use an ability he had as a child: to be able to imagine a thing as it is in reality, quick as lightning, and believe in it.[39]

This is, of course, the same demand that is placed on the reader of any of Vesaas' written works, but in the radio play the proper use of sounds and pauses is an extra aid with which the listener is provided. This is perhaps also at least a partial explanation of why Vesaas' radio plays have always been so much more successful than his stage plays. In the theater, the spectator has the scene as Vesaas and the director have imagined it in full view before him on the stage, and is thus deprived of the opportunity to create his own version of it in his own mind, but it is precisely this that he is required to do when listening to a radio play, and which Vesaas' evocative images help him to do.

The radio play is also the ideal expressive medium for Vesaas' ability to say things between the lines. He also discusses this point in the same article:

> And [the lines] must be given time to come to life and affect the listener before the next lines come and quench them. It depends on the play, but the pacing is often too quick. Nowhere else can small pauses be so filled with speech as in a radio play.[40]

Vesaas employs these same techniques just as successfully in "Blue Button Lost," which also was originally a radio play (1956) before appearing in short story form in *One Fine Day*. It is very close in its theme to "Mist Rain": the hesitancy and apprehension before sexual experience and maturity. In the radio play form there was the same evocative use of sounds: the roar of an automobile engine, the sound of sudden, sharp rain showers, a motorboat off at a distance, and the same tension-filled use of pauses. There are deeper perspectives in the delineation of the conflicts than in "Mist Rain," however. Not only the relationships between the young girl who is the main character and the two boys she is trying to choose between are investigated, but also those between the girl and the other members of her family, and especially her brother, are treated with great sensitivity.

II   Spring Night

Some of the same situations and conflicts, and many more in addition, are discussed in the novel *Spring Night* (*Vårnatt*, 1954). In this novel it is the brother who is the central figure, but his relationship to his sister and her emotional situation plays an important part in the development of the story and in his own emotional development.

Spring Night is the story of fourteen-year-old Hallstein and his eighteen-year-old sister Sissel who are alone at home while their parents are away for the night.

When the reader first meets Hallstein, he is a quite typical fourteen-year-old boy, still occupied with his world of daydreams and fantasies, unsure of himself and confused by the many new feelings he is experiencing. He has a fantasy girl friend whom he calls Gudrun and who appears to him in the attic window when he raps on the wall of the house. He confides in her and, although he realizes how ridiculous it all is, takes comfort in the way she understands him and his problems. Gudrun resembles his sister a little, especially in the way they laugh, and Hallstein has been spying on Sissel and her boyfriend sitting listening to the radio together as the novel opens. He feels guilty, but is fascinated, watching them teasing and bickering. He finds a release for his confused feelings by retreating into his make-believe world of conversations with Gudrun and the hypnotic trances he puts himself into imagining the presence of a snake that were discussed in Chapter 1. At the same time, however, he is in close contact with nature, and feels strongly possessive of it. His favorite spot is a fertile hillside in the woods near the house:

The slope was covered by a whole forest of angelica. It was half turned from the sun, but the plants thrived in the slanting evening sun and the raw earth. Although it was yet early in the summer, the angelica had already begun to assume its stately form, rigidly lovely in its burst of life. It was all Hallstein's, it was he who had shaken the seed out and then trodden it into the earth.[41]

This description of the fecund glade of angelica where Hallstein has his snake fantasies is typical of the rich, lyrical nature descriptions in so much of Vesaas' writing during the 1950's, but which often, as in this case, go far beyond mere nature description. The difficulties which Hallstein is experiencing in releasing his grip on his childhood world, for example, are also well presented in his attitude toward the snails which come out in the hollow behind the house in expectation of rain later that evening. He and Sissel go down there together to see them:

> They lay down on the ground. The grass was cool and felt good against their skin. In front of them lay a couple of huge snails. Lay in quiet rest and stretched themselves out, coal black, apparently lifeless, but Sissel and Hallstein knew that they were being scrutinized.
> They did not say a word. There was no sound—except for the lazy humming of a car somewhere on the road. A reminder that the ordinary world was not far away. But the snails lay glistening and black on a light green carpet and just existed. They were Hallstein's snails, he had made an agreement with his father about it when he was four years old. For ten years he had had a feeling of ownership—it would be difficult to grow out of it.[42]

Hallstein and Sissel sit together in the warm, humid evening, waiting for the rain to begin and wanting to talk to each other about their problems, but without being able to. When the rain does come, it is as a relief:

> The raindrops came down harder and heavier. It began to affect the snails, but just as a new pleasure, a small movement in something on one end—they had senses open for the heaven's rain.[43]

Hallstein and Sissel are just as open to the world of nature around them, and are affected by it as much as the snails are. They are even able to communicate with each other, wordlessly but totally, under its influence:

> The rain was so warm that it was good to feel it on a sunburned body—there was not the least need to seek shelter. . . . They sat and let the warm shower of rain wash them, tousle them a bit, too, externally, but only externally: their hair, the small plastered-on garments, their cheeks—internally they blossomed under it.
> Blossomed; why? No way to know. No way to ask. They sat side by side and shared a thousand small memories. Sat motionless.[44]

They finally go home, change clothes and prepare for a nice evening alone together:

No one had promised them that, it just hung in the air. They did not talk about it, just felt it in everything: the security and the freedom at the same time. All that had happened down in the hollow. The strange, tempting feelings. It was something to sit peacefully with—just the two of them in a tranquility.[45]

Before they even have a chance to eat supper, however, a knock comes at the door and their peaceful, if at times confusing, world is invaded by a group of people in contact with whom both Hallstein and Sissel are changed, and their conception of the world altered forever. The group of people is a family consisting of a father, Hjalmar, and his two children: a thirteen-year-old daughter, Gudrun, and a married son, Karl, whose wife, Grete, is about to have a baby. Their old car has broken down on the road below the house, and they are seeking shelter and help. Still down in the car is Hjalmar's second wife, Kristine, with whom he has no children.

Hjalmar and his children and wife are all more or less neurotic. Gudrun, whose sudden appearance seems to Hallstein to be an incarnation of his dreams, is the least disturbed of them, but even she is nervous and unpredictable. Karl is highstrung and given to sudden, violent outbursts, and his father, Hjalmar, is close to being a nervous wreck. He is constantly moving and talking, and drives nearly everyone around him to distraction. But it is Kristine whose psychological state is the most critical. The relationship between her and Hjalmar, which has apparently been strained for a long time, has come to the stage where she refuses to speak to him as a result of his having wished she were dumb. No explanation of why their relationship is so poor is given to the reader or to Hallstein, who merely sees, and reacts to, the situation as it is at the moment. Kristine speaks to Hallstein, however; at first in the car when they are there alone, and later when they are alone together in the house. She is also lame, and has to be carried everywhere by Hjalmar and Karl. Hallstein is plagued by his suspicion, which grows to near certainty, that her lameness is only feigned, but he never expresses it. Her condition is not really feigned, however. She tells Hallstein:

"If someone stood over me with an axe, I still couldn't say a word if I knew it would reach his ears. It's that bad."[46]

Hallstein is both frightened and fascinated by the woman. He first realizes how sick she is when she tells him:

"It's getting closer and closer around me. Do you think it's any fun to see the walls come creeping in from all sides?"[47]

Kristine is one of Vesaas' most chilling, and at the same time convincing, portraits of people shut off from contact with others, as exaggerated as her condition sounds at first. It is as an intermediary in the psychological struggle raging between Kristine and Hjalmar that Hallstein feels the greatest pressure put on him. They both demand that he help them, and he is at a loss to know how to meet these apparently contradictory demands on his loyalty. Also Grete and Karl ask for his help. After the baby has been born and everyone quartered in various rooms in the house, Hallstein wanders from room to room, visiting one after the other. Grete, who feels that now that Karl has a child things will be easier for him and that this will affect the others, asks Hallstein to go up to the attic where Karl is and keep him company. Hallstein is a bit afraid of Karl, but carries out Grete's errand, and discovers that Karl does indeed need help, and that he can provide it. He also visits Gudrun, who is in his room, lying naked in his own bed. The scene between them is bursting with latent sexuality which they can express only indirectly. In their excitement and embarrassment and confusion they decide to measure arms:

They put their arms together and placed their fingertips against each other's shoulders. It was strange. This is something big, Hallstein thought. They forgot to decide whose arm was longest.

They could do no more. They were speechless and serious. It was quickly over.

"Put it under the blanket again," Hallstein said—he felt he had to say that, no matter how little he wished it.

"It's not cold," she answered.

"No, not at all. It's warm enough to go naked, for that matter," he stammered out.

Gudrun brought her left arm out, too. Hallstein saw that the two arms were infinitely beautiful. He did not try to touch them. Neither of them mentioned anything about seeing more.[48]

In contact with all these people Hallstein learns a great deal about the demands that life can make on a person, and also about the tensions that can arise in interpersonal relationships. This is expressed in a fine image of the house and its rooms which comes to his mind:

Once out in the yard, Hallstein had to look up at the yellow wall of the house—in wonder that it still looked the same—now that every one of its rooms was occupied by unexpected and unimaginable things. It occurred to him that he could have felt it trembling if he had placed his hand on it. An incredible night. From every room came calls to him, and he had to go in.[49]

This tension is broken, and partially alleviated, by Kristine's sudden death, apparently as the result of a heart attack when the old car crashes into the side of the house near the room where she is sleeping. It is Hjalmar who, although he cannot drive, brings this about while he is attempting to fix the car. Her death is made less tragic thas it might otherwise have been by the birth of the child just a few hours before, and by Karl's reassuring his father that he had done all he could for Kristine by the way in which he had carried her uncomplainingly for so long.

Hallstein can hardly believe that these things are really happening in his house, and he attempts several times during the night to dismiss it all as a dream, but realizes that he has to accept it as reality. He realizes also that his world of fantasy has been shattered forever, and that his dream girl Gudrun will never again appear in the attic window. It is not his ability to dream which has been weakened, however, but his ability to accept reality which has been strengthened. This is beautifully expressed by a vision he has as they are returning to the house after taking Kristine to the hospital:

Tonight, today anything can happen. When we get home, maybe the yellow house won't be there. We come to where it used to be, but there's only a large graceful angelica standing there bristling in the wind. A soft breeze is blowing, because the house had stood just there.

Sissel peeks out from behind the angelica. Is so small that she can hide behind a flower now.

No one can come here, she says.

But what about mother and father and the house?

And Karl steps forward:

Yes, and all I had here? Grete, and a litle star that was mine?

They receive no answer.

Hallstein stands with Gudrun beside the huge angelica and tells her all he knows about angelica—[50]

But Hallstein realizes that this is only a fantasy and is ready to accept the reality of the situation:

> When they came to the bottom of the hill the house stood on, the house was standing there all right. More solid than in any dream.[51]

An important undercurrent in the development of the plot is the changing relationship between Hallstein and Sissel. He is very attached to her, and at the beginning of the novel jealous of her boyfriend, Tore. During the night Sissel is very strongly attracted to Karl, and although Hallstein doesn't actually understand what it is, he somehow senses that she is changing, as is indicated by the role she plays in his vision of the house disappearing. Several times during the night he also runs into Tore, who is wandering around in the rain-soaked birch groves surrounding the house. Aided by his own developing feelings for the real Gudrun, Hallstein gradually experiences Tore less and less as a threat, and by the time morning comes is able to accept that Sissel will be Tore's without feeling any animosity toward him. This does not change back even after Hallstein realizes that he does not mean to Gudrun what she means to him, and that he will never see her again. His change has been an irreversible one, and he has taken an important step along the road to maturity. The symbolic significance for Hallstein's life of the many tumultuous events of the night is underlined by Karl's last words to him as they all drive off: "Maybe we'll meet again when you're grown up."[52]

One of the reasons that it is possible for Hallstein to mature as successfully as he does under the pressures that are put on him is that he is "normal," that is, he has the emotional and intellectual potential to develop, and he is not hindered by his circumstances from developing. Vesaas has written extensively about people who are in one way or the other abnormal, principally about those who are hindered psychologically from developing relationships to others, such as Klas Dyregodt, who overcomes his difficulties, and Jorunn in *The Tower*, who does not. Another group of abnormal persons, those who lack the intellectual or emotional potential to develop, has also been of interest to Vesaas throughout his entire writing career. In each of his first three collections of short stories there is a story dealing at least partially with a mentally retarded person.

III   *"The Stunted Spruce"*

During the war Vesaas wrote, but did not publish, a story which was first titled "The Stunted Spruce," but which when it appeared in *The Winds* had the title "The Half-Wit." The background for this story was, according to Vesaas, a remark he happened to overhear in 1933: "—stunted spruces on a marsh can give you a lot to think about."[53] Such stunted spruces play an important role in the story, where they represent the undeveloped aspects of the story's main character, a mentally retarded man. His personality and his attitude toward the world, and the world's attitude toward him, are succinctly described in the opening paragraphs of the story:

Mattis was stopped in the middle of the road and asked whether he could take on some woodcutting. A big tall man was standing in front of him, looking him straight in the eye.

"What?" said Mattis in confusion. He couldn't believe he'd heard quite right. Sometimes he was bothered by a ringing in his ears. But— hadn't the man called him by name?

The man repeated:

"I just asked if you could take on some woodcutting for me, Mattis."

Mattis, he had said, just like that. As if he were speaking to one of the regular work-hands.

Mattis felt a warm wave of joy wash over him. But he was careful to hide it from the man. Everyday work-hands wouldn't get all upset over being asked such a question, he knew. They'd just answer calmly yes or no, whichever fitted best. But this big, impressive man had said *Mattis.* And everybody who called him Mattis got a sort of star fastened to him, right then and there. If people spoke to him at all, they hardly ever called him by name. He knew very well that behind his back they called him "the half-wit."

"Yes," he said, after getting all this sorted out inside his skull.[54]

On his way home after he has finished talking with the man Mattis walks past a marsh:

A wide, dank, wild marsh with an occasional spruce-clump sprawling in the moss. Small stunted spruce that never matured. They barely hung on to life, and were covered with nothing but lichens and gnarly dried-up twigs.

There they were again—

Mattis looked uneasily at them.[55]

Mattis lives with his older sister, Hege, who supports them both with her knitting. She is pleased at the prospect of his making a little money, and sends him off the next day to the forest on the other side of the lake where he is to chop. When he is in the woods alone, Mattis is quite a different person. He responds extremely sensitively to the total environment of the forest:

> ... he became aware of everything around him with a strange, secret clarity. There was a smell of spices and greenery here, from the glistening and swaying tree-tops and from new grass. White anemone was growing on the forest floor, and was on the verge of going to seed. From the birchwood he was chopping came a faint fragrance which he took part in—so fresh that it suggested the fragrance of spring moistness. He saw snails climb on the wood and look around with friendly eyes on stalks. A thrush called in a fir-top. There was joy in every single thing—he sensed it and understood it and was part of it.
> He felled a huge birch in this moment of joy. First he felt a shower of raindrops on his back when the tree shivered before it fell. Then came the fall, and the sighing of the leaves through the web of rain. That's the way I'll sigh when I die, he thought suddenly. This is the sighing through my own heart.
> Mattis looked around to see whether anyone had heard this last thought—he had thought it out loud. He was trembling with joy over having been able to think such things. He wished that wise people had heard that. He said it again: This is the sighing through my own heart.[56]

This ecstatic moment doesn't last, however. He grows physically tired, and the sight of some stunted spruce in a nearby marsh depresses him:

> The stunted trees cast their shadow into the very heart of his sacred birch-forest. He was weak and drained after the ecstasy of a moment ago, and the hollowness within him was filled with dread. He couldn't take his eyes from the stunted spruce no matter what, and when he wanted to continue chopping, he could scarcely manage to lift the axe.[57]

The dread which Mattis feels at the sight of the stunted spruce is connected with the fact that he had earlier chopped down one of them in anger and frustration at his own lack of strength and his inability to do a decent day's work. Mattis has a tendency to think in terms of similes, and to see signs and omens in all sorts

of events and everyday happenings that "normal" people gener-
aly take at face value. It is not difficult for him to sense that
his act of chopping down the stunted spruce is connected with his
own fate, is in a sense a symbolic suicide. He thus connects his
own death with this act, as well as with his chopping down of
the birch trees. Mattis feels a strong sense of identification with
trees, and this motif appears again in *The Birds* (*Fuglane*), the
novel published in 1957 which deals in greater detail with Mattis
and his world.

IV The Birds

In the novel, Mattis is presented to the reader in the same way
as in the short story, with one difference. He is less frequently
referred to as "the half-wit," and then only when it is clear that
it is an expression of the attitude of other people toward him.
Even the tree with which he identifies, and with which he is
identified, in the novel bears his real name:

Just beyond the fence stood two withered aspen trees, their bare,
white tops jutting up among the green spruces. They stood close to
each other, and among people in the village they were called *Mattis-
and-Hege*, though not openly. It was only by accident that Mattis
had got to hear the names. . . .
Two withered aspen trees side by side, in among the green growing
spruces.[58]

This is a striking image of Mattis and his life, and he realizes
this himself, but thinks it is unfair that Hege is included:

He was angry, too, that Hege had been compared to a withered tree
top, it was nothing like her! Surely anyone could see that. Hege, who
was so clever and wise.
What is it that hurts so much?
You know very well, came the reply, somehow meaningless, yet
straight to the point.[59]

The truth of the situation, which Mattis has difficulty admitting
to himself, is that it is he, Mattis, who is to blame for Hege being
included in the ridicule aimed at him. He realizes also that he is
at least partially to blame for her state of loneliness and the fact,
which he discovers in the opening pages of the novel, that she is
getting gray hair although she is only forty years old. It is his
feeling of shame over all this that hurts so much.

This is typical for Mattis. He is extremely sensitive to the emotional states of other people, even though he may not be able to understand clearly why they are that way. He has difficulty pinning down the reason that Hege sometimes cries at night, but he senses that its cause has something to do with him. He cannot fully understand the behavior of a young girl in love whom he meets, but he can sense her joyous condition, and derive joy from it himself. Mattis' sensitivity to nature is as central to *The Birds* as to "The Stunted Spruce." In the novel it is expressed mainly by one of the most beautiful images in all of Vesaas' writing: that of the mating track of the woodcock.

One evening when Mattis is sitting outside and looking out over the forest surrounding their little house, he hears a tiny sound:

All of a sudden a strange cry, and at the same time he could just make out quick flapping wings in the air above him. Then came more faint calls in a helpless bird language.
It went straight across the house.[60]

The significance of this for Mattis is described in an extension of the image:

Mattis looked at his house. It seemed to be a different house now, you had to look at it with different eyes. The woodcock had always seemed to be something that glided through valleys far away from all that was his. That was how he had always imagined it. Now, this evening, it was here, it had simply moved right here.[61]

The woodcock track represents for Mattis something that is distant and unattainable, something he had never dreamed could be his. He sees in its moving a sign that things will be different from then on, but he doesn't know in what way. He believes he finds the answer to this in a dream he has that same night. The dream is of clearly erotic nature, and this is in keeping with the natural function of the mating track of the bird. He dreams that he is changed in three ways: he is sexually attractive, he is intelligent and can say witty things, and he is strong.

For Mattis the coming of the track of the woodcock is the most important event of his life, and he is shocked and confused by Hege's indifference when he tells her about it:

"Didn't you hear what I said? There's a woodcock here! It's moved its track! It's flying straight across the roof of our house! Now! This very minute, while you're sitting there in bed."

Hege remained sitting as before, with the same expression on her face.

"Of course I heard. But what of it? Can't you let the woodcock come and go as it likes?"

He didn't understand her. It was as if she were speaking a language he didn't understand.[62]

One of Mattis' greatest problems is his inability to communicate with those around him, even with Hege, his own sister. Not only can he not express himself in words, but he is not even able to use his experience of nature to make himself understood, as Hallstein in *Spring Night* is able to do. Mattis, cut off from communication with other human beings, is reduced to communicating with nature, and it is thus not surprising that he identifies with objects in nature rather than with other people. This sense of identification reaches its peak in Mattis' relationship to the woodcock. Time and again he connects himself and the woodcock in his mind: "The woodcock and me, sort of," and these words are almost a refrain running through the novel. And it is with the woodcock that he attains communication. One day he walks past a dried-up mud hole in the woods beneath the woodcock's track:

In the smooth brown surface of the marshy soil were the light imprints of a bird's feet. A number of tiny, deep round holes had been dug as well. The woodcock had been there. The deep holes had been made by the woodcock's beak which it thrust down into the ground to dig up morsels of food, or sometimes just to prick out messages.

Mattis bent down and read what was written. Looked at the graceful dancing footprints. That's how fine and graceful the bird is, he thought. That's how gracefully my bird walks over the marshy ground when he's tired of the air.

You are you, that was what was written.

What a greeting to receive!

He found a twig and pricked an answer in an empty space on the brown surface. He didn't use ordinary letters; it was meant for the woodcock, so he wrote in the same way as the birds. . . .

Tomorrow he would come back and see how the woodcock had got on with reading it. He went home whistling to himself, but said nothing—Hege was shut off from understanding things like this.[63]

Mattis communicates with the woodcock in this way for several days, and the tragedy of his situation is intensified by his own realization of it:

> He would have liked to have started using bird language for good—to have gone back home to Hege and never spoken in any other way. Then she might have begun to understand some of the things that were at present hidden from her.
> But he didn't dare, he had a fair idea of what would happen. Most likely they'd lock me up. They'd refuse to have anything to do with the finest of all languages, they'd laugh at it.[64]

Mattis and Hallstein resemble each other in many more ways than their close contact with nature. They are both emotionally immature and are both attached to their older sisters. They both live in a dream world which is closely connected with their apprehension of nature, but there is an important difference between them: Hallstein is capable of developing emotionally when life demands it, but Mattis is not. This difference between them is illustrated in *The Birds* by Mattis' reaction to two events.

The first of these is the shooting of the woodcock. Mattis mentions the flight of the woodcock to a young boy, and realizes too late that he has sealed the bird's fate. He attempts to dismiss it all as a dream, just as Hallstein tries to do, but the dead body of the bird, which he buries beneath a stone, is proof of the opposite. Although he realizes this, he still cannot accept it, and continues to identify with the bird, and with its fate:

> Down on the shore Mattis had many new thoughts—they were about eyes under stones: There's lid upon lid and stone upon stone, but it can never be hidden.
> The surface of the lake stretched into the distance. He looked out across it. Dimly he thought: help Mattis.
> Why!
> He gave a start.
> No, no, he mumbled meaninglessly, and seized the oars.
> Lead in the wing, he thought, and there's stone upon stone, over the eyes.[65]

The other event which has a crucial effect on Mattis' life is the coming of Jörgen, with whom Hege falls in love. Just as Mattis had, in a sense, brought about the death of the woodcock by telling the boy about it, he also brings about the change in Hege's life which has such tragic results for him. Although he is incapable of doing any sort of productive work, Mattis is a brilliant rower. No one can compete with him in rowing a straight line, and he spends much time on the lake in his boat. There is some danger in this, since he cannot swim, but it is the only thing that he can do that gives him satisfaction. Hege, in an attempt to keep him busy, suggests one day that he become a ferryman, and ferry people across the lake, even though there is no one living on the other side. He seizes upon the idea immediately, and starts ferrying. On the very first day it just so happens that a lumberman comes hiking through the woods on the other side of the lake, and Mattis does actually get a passenger—his only one. He brings the lumberman, Jörgen, home with him. Jörgen finds work in the woods nearby and stays. Just as Hallstein loses his sister to another, Mattis loses Hege, but he is not able to make the emotional adjustment demanded of him. Jörgen tries to teach him to cut timber so that he can earn his own keep, but he is unsuccessful. Hege, also unsuccessfully, tries to explain her needs to him, and to encourage and help him to accept the situation. Mattis is unable to mature enough to be able to give his sister the freedom she has a right to.

He realizes he is only in the way, and that Hege would be better off without him, but he is incapable of making a decision to act to remove himself from her life. He is, however, able to devise an ingenious plan which will leave the decision to other forces. He decides to row out on the lake on a still day, kick a hole in the bottom of his boat, and float on the oars. If the weather remains calm, he can manage to get to shore; if not, he will die. He waits many days for the right weather, rows far out to a spot in the lake where no one can see him, puts his plan into effect, and delivers himself into the hands of fate:

Mattis pushed himself forwards, was staring fixedly at a point on the western slopes. The point nearest to him. He must plough his way through the water with every ounce of strength he could muster—that was part of the plan.

A puff of air moved across the lake after a while, as if someone had breathed on it. Here and there a shadow landed on the surface, but Mattis didn't notice. He struggled and gasped for air and went on pushing himself slowly forwards in the same direction. In the meantime a bank of cloud had risen over the horizon—he didn't see that either. . . .

"Hege!" he shouted all of a sudden—he had seen the wind coming. So the wind was coming after all! The gentle breath of air had quickly changed to wind. In the distance Mattis could see a dark-blue line stretching right across the surface of the water, and his face turned pale. It was quickly moving nearer. Blue and strong the wind sped from the clouds behind him—soon the lake would be in a turmoil.

Already the wind was whipping up white crests on the waves; they would soon fill Mattis' mouth with water and rob him of breath. Before long he would lose the oars.

"Mattis!" he shouted in his confusion and utter helplessness. Across the desolate water his cry sounded like the call of a strange bird. How big or small that bird was, you couldn't really tell.[66]

The tragedy of Mattis is not merely the tragedy of a mentally retarded man living in a rural village; it is the tragedy of every person who at one time or another finds it impossible to communicate with others. Fortunately for most people, this is not a permanent condition, such as it is for Mattis, and they are able to survive the periods of isolation which they experience. This is at least partially due to the fact that society is more lenient in its judgment of those who do not display the types of deficiencies Mattis is encumbered with, although they may have other deficiencies which are just as serious. Mattis' tragedy is not so much that he does not possess the abilities and skills which society demands that he have, but rather that society is so structured that it has difficulty in taking advantage of the abilities and gifts which he does possess. It is possible to see all sorts of human types in the portrait of Mattis in *The Birds*: the dreamer, the poet, the eternal child, the visionary, the mystic, depending upon how the novel is read, and all these interpretations are certainly valid. But Mattis is above all a human being who has a right to be accepted as he is by his fellow human beings. It also seems clear that society has a need of those who display those gifts which are Mattis'. It will find itself in great danger the day there is no longer anyone who can understand the significance and importance of a woodcock's flight over the house.

CHAPTER 7

Problems of Isolation and Involvement
1959-1968

THE LAST two stories in the collection *One Fine Day*, published in 1959, two years after the publication of *The Birds*, distinguish themselves quite sharply from the other stories in that collection. Although they contain no motifs or stylistic features which are not also to be found in other works by Vesaas up to that time, they represent nevertheless a major change in attitude and technique. The first, and shortest, of these two stories, "Three Quiet Men," served as the basis for the discussion of Vesaas' literary technique in Chapter 1 of this book. The other, "Snow," is slightly more than twice as long as "Three Quiet Men," but is still the next-to-shortest story in the collection. It is also written in a highly concentrated, expressionistic style which places great demands on the reader's ability to associate and invest the images presented to him with meaning. It is closely related thematically to *The Birds*, being also a study of extreme isolation and lack of contact, and can similarly be interpreted in many different ways. The image presented in the opening paragraphs is an arresting one:

Snow is falling over the plains—in a vast wilderness. Not a living tree. A single house is standing here. It will become smaller for each passing hour, and be snowed under.

Drifts are piling up around the house. Stars are quietly and lightly settling on the roof. No weight at all—but finally the roof-beams will give way under the crushing pressure.[1]

There is a single man in the house, and he feels the weight of the snow settling on the roof above him:

Play! he shouts, and the room plays. The music is he himself—it is the only thing that is of use in the battle with the stars. But in order to get music he must take, piece by piece, that which he has within himself and with which he shall save himself.[2]

Although this man and this house are isolated now, this has not always been the case:

138

The sustaining strings that once were connected have been cut off, one by one. Where are the hidden scissors? He does not know. He knows very little. But he is holding out.[3]

I The Fire

This theme of broken contact, and the plight of those affected by it, is central to the novel *The Fire* (*Brannen*), which was published in 1961 and was Vesaas' first novel following the publication of "Three Quiet Men" and "Snow." It resembles these stories in its use of startling images and anti-realistic elements, and the result of employing these techniques in the full novel form is the creation of a hypnotic, dreamlike atmosphere. In this novel the development toward abstraction in character portrayal in Vesaas' novels between 1940 and 1950 is brought to its culmination. Only the main character is named, but even the name given him is as unspecific as possible: Jon. All the other characters whom Jon meets, and in terms of whom Jon's personality is revealed to the reader, have only descriptive titles: the man sawing in the woods, the woman from the cauldron of sheep, the truck driver, the owner of the meadow, etc.

Jon's situation in life is sketched quickly in the first few pages of the novel: he has just finished his studies, has taken a job, and moved into a room in a town where he knows no one. His unsuccessful attempts to establish a lasting emotional relationship are summed up in a few brief flashbacks. One of the girls with whom he has broken gives a succinct characterization of him:

"You don't *see* anything. You only see your papers and studies. Rattling paper is just paper to me. There are other things in life."[4]

Of all the characters in Vesaas' other books Jon thus resembles most closely the stamp collector Martin in *The House in Darkness*, at least at the beginning of *The Fire*. In contrast to Martin, however, Jon does not retreat into total isolation when life places demands on him. He is, in fact, aware that demands will be made of him and is anxiously awaiting them when the novel opens. He is staring at the telephone in his room and wondering who will be the first to call him:

The line is open. Open to everything.
It would be natural that a girl would be the first person to call me,

he thought, and tried in this way to make the telephone enticing. A
girl calling a fellow.

No use.

Open to everything.

That's what it was.

Shut it out.

No. You're not that afraid.

Open on all sides.

Suddenly he realized something: the callers. People who are confused and bewildered.

They never stop calling, he thought. People are calling from everywhere. He had thought about it often, but now it flared up and he felt
weak. They're after me, he thought. I've seen them.

At that moment the telephone rang.

Jon started. The sound cut through to the marrow.

Ring as much as you want. I'll just let it ring.

If you don't answer you'll be marked by it for life.

He picked up the telephone and called softly:

"Hello."

A voice at the other end said, as if choked by smoke:

"It's a call from my home!"

The receiver clicked, the call was cut off. Or choked by smoke.[5]

This call does succeed in calling Jon out, into contact with
"people who are confused and bewildered." It is clear from this
passage that Jon's fate is in his own hands, and like Klas Dyregodt he realizes it. It is he himself who is shutting himself off
from life, both from its pleasant and its unpleasant aspects, and
it is only he who can open himself to it. The use of the pronoun
"my" in the telephone message underlines that it is also he himself who is calling himself out, and that the journey he is about
to set out on is an inner journey. This is made even clearer
toward the end of the novel when Jon thinks: "It was as if everything he had seen had been himself."[6]

What he sees in the course of the novel, the many and varied
experiences he has, clearly reveals to Jon how difficult, but also
rewarding, life can be for those who dare to participate in it. The
description of the telephone message also gives a forewarning of
the central image of the book: that of fire. In this novel, as in
most of Vesaas' production, fire is both a creative and a destructive force. It is a force which is within human beings, and which
must be reckoned with. *The Fire* can indeed be looked upon as
being an exegesis of a line from the poem "The Living," in the

collection *The Land of Hidden Fires*, which expresses this idea in highly concentrated form: "The fire dwells in man and is there to stay."

As soon as he steps out of the door of his house Jon meets a girl who suggests they go for a walk together. They walk along silently for a while, but no deeper contact is established. He feels that the girl is frightened, but is unable to approach her, and they part in silence. His next experience is less equivocal, but no less confusing. Suddenly a little boy grabs his hand and tells him he has to come with him to his father. Jon follows him without realizing what the purpose of his meeting the boy's father is, and soon finds himself face to face with one of Vesaas' most compelling and disturbing portraits of the obsessed personality. The boy's father is sawing in the woods. The boy tells Jon about it:

> "We keep sawing night and day, as long as he can hold out."
> "Why?"
> The boy's answer was like a burning whisper:
> "I don't know."[7]

When Jon arrives at the clearing in the woods where the father is sawing he discovers that the forest floor is covered with shining discs of wood that the man has cut, and which light up the dark forest. The boy seizes each one as soon as it has been cut from the felled tree, and strews them around. The man sawing is hostile to Jon's presence, and quickly sends him on his way again. He also asks Jon two questions which he cannot answer satisfactorily: "Have you ever been in the fire?"[8] and "What do you know about all this?"[9] Jon leaves, but feels he has somehow failed in this meeting. Though disheartened, he continues his journey, with the sound of the sawing always present in the background and his synthesis of the man's questions constantly in mind: What do I know about fire?

Many of the other people Jon meets are also in the hands of obsessive or self-destructive forces. His next meeting is with a woman who turns out to be the mother of the girl Jon had walked with, and who shows him a horrible sight: a pile of sheep trapped in a cleft in the mountains, suffocating in the heat radiating from the steep rock walls enclosing them. She tells him that she has done this, and has to show someone what it is like to be her. Jon flees in terror and confusion, but there are still worse things in store for him. He hitches a ride with a truck driver who smashes his truck into a house by the roadside, killing a man inside. He takes part in a nightmarish race along dark roads in the middle of the night and a frightening walk with two other men through a narrow valley filled with low bushes which one of the men imagines are infested with snakes. He comes upon the man sawing several more times, and the last time they meet the man tells him that the boy has disappeared down into the forest floor beneath the slices of wood.

Not all of Jon's experiences are of this kind, however. He meets the young girl again several times, and although he is now hindered from approaching her by what he knows about her mother, these meetings are still good experiences for him. He overhears a lovers' tryst in a meadow over-ripe for cutting and watches while frost-chilled swallows are carried into a shed and resuscitated. During all these experiences the sawing man's questions are replaced in Jon's mind by the thought: It can be like this, too. Of all these good experiences the one that means the most for Jon is being allowed to take part in a search party looking for a missing girl. Jon has heard a girl's voice calling out in the darkness of the night, and has tried to find her on his own, but unsuccessfully. The search party also fails to find her, but in the novel's final episode Jon does stumble over her, and although it is too late to save the girl this experience has a final positive effect on Jon's development, and at the end of his inner journey Jon realizes he must, and is able to, be concerned about and involved in the fate of others.

Thematically, *The Fire* is closer to the Dyregodt novels than to any other books by Vesaas. The development that Jon undergoes parallels rather closely that of Klas', although the techniques employed to describe the developments in the two works are quite different. In keeping with the general technical development in Vesaas' writing in the 1940's and 1950's, the exposition of the theme of development from a state of isolation to one of involvement is much less realistic and more abstract in *The Fire* than in the Dyregodt novels. This is revealed in several ways in addition to the extreme lack of individualization in character portrayal. The manner in which Jon receives encouragement to continue his journey, for example, involves several incidents which contrast rather sharply with the scenes in which Klas receives advice and encouragement from specific people.

After having witnessed the death of the truck driver, Jon wanders into the woods in the middle of the night and leans up against what he believes to be a tree. After a while, however, he realizes that he is leaning against another man's back:

> Jon waited impatiently. That man behind him should say something! But the silence remained unbroken, and that was good, too— it didn't matter. But the silence was impossible. To move was impossible. But that was good, too. Say something. No, no! Jon held his breath and listened. Heard nothing. The man sawing? he thought. He must still be sawing. No, there was no sound of sawing. It was peaceful here.[10]

This contact, fleeting and unspecific as it is, is of great help to Jon. It is immediately after he has left the man in the woods that he takes part in the eerie race through the night, and realizes what the purpose of his search for himself is:

> The great goal: what have I done with my heart, my mind, and with the darkness.[11]

Another moment of fleeting contact has a significant effect on Jon. While stumbling through the darkness earlier that same night he is on the point of stepping into a bottomless mud hole at the edge of a marsh, but is saved when he steps on a marsh hen crouching in the grass. He never sees the bird, but hears her and her chicks scuttling around in the darkness. He is grateful that she was there, and when he rises to leave he very carefully feels around him in the darkness so as not to injure the hen or her chicks. It is the first time that Jon shows true concern and consideration for other living things; it is an important turning point in his development.

One of the most interesting points of comparison between *The Fire* and the Dyregodt novels, and one which illustrates well the abstract nature of the imagery in *The Fire,* is the scene in which Jon is most directly brought face to face with death. As in the Dyregodt books, this takes place in an empty hay barn. Jon has just finished talking with the owner of the over-ripe meadow which is being mown, and the man is depressed. Jon agrees to wait for him in the old barn beside the meadow:

A little while later the barn began to tremble. Jon felt it as soon as it began. He had been sitting hunched up in the empty hay mow. What's that trembling? There was no one to ask; he had to keep it to himself.

He realized that he himself was shaking too. You who have landed right in the middle of it, and will never have any more peace.[12]

He later discovers that while he had been waiting, the owner of the meadow had died. Whereas in the Dyregodt books it is natural forces (wind, water) which cause structures to tremble, and in *The House in Darkness* it is a symbolic storm that is raging, in *The Fire* the cause of the trembling is unspecified and totally abstract. Jon later in the same passage imagines that the wind is blowing, but the trembling comes from forces inside Jon himself, and this is in keeping with the whole structure of the novel.

That the entire novel is an inner revelation is made clear in the final episode. Jon has just left the shed where the frost-numbed swallows are being revived, and has been filled with joy at this sight. He walks through the countryside:

Jon left the open country and walked through woods and groves. The frost hadn't struck there. He went farther in; he went farther down. There was no road there leading through the dells.[13]

This final and decisive journey into the uncharted depths within himself results in Jon's finding the lost girl everyone has been searching for. She is close to death when he finds her, and there is little he can do to help her. He attempts to carry her away, but she resists. She tells him that she is doing what she is to show other people "what life can be like."[14] Even though she resists his efforts to help her, she says that she is glad that he has come, since he can now tell others about it, and her efforts won't be wasted. She demands that he promise to do so, and although Jon still cannot understand why it is necessary for her to die, he promises. He immediately feels this promise as a burden, but realizes he has to take it upon himself. The girl's death has a final, strongly positive effect on Jon:

Wreathed in the silver-gray dew of morning he stands in the deepest dell. So much a part of the bushes that he is as nothing.

The vault of space is immense. An icy coldness pours down from it. A radiance pours down from it. It is overwhelming, as it arches above him.

In his eyes the earth arches to meet it, bowl-shaped from horizon to horizon, with the deepest dell in the middle, gently rising on all sides.

No one in sight throughout the huge arching of the earth—except a little speck of a dead girl lying in the deepest dell, wreathed in the morning dew and sleep. Just a speck—but still the only thing there. The first bitter hour passes. The next bitter hour begins.

What do you do now?

Have you seen the mirrors turn, so that you know who you are? What you are?

The morning grows stronger. Space pours down its distant radiance. What next. Signals will pass through the huge vault. From the deepest dell. Just a speck in an immense arching. But still—[15]

In this final scene of the novel the description of the development Jon has undergone is complete. Like Knut in "Last Man Home," "his senses are open like a bowl," and he is prepared to receive everything, both good and bad, that life has to offer him. More than that, he is prepared to become involved in life and with the lives of other people, and he has accomplished this, as did also Klas Dyregodt, by actively facing up to life situations and learning through practice what involvement means and entails. It is also quite clear from this final scene that one of the crucial stages in Jon's development has also been that of self-discovery:

Have you seen the mirrors turn, so that you know who you are? What you are?

Just before Jon descends into "the deepest dell" another image of self-examination is used:

He walked along, staring into his own eye. What is this? Who are you? *Are* you all this?[16]

Jon also experiences an examining eye outside of himself. He is walking through the countryside the evening of the night of frost during which the swallows are paralyzed by the cold:

Frost was in the air. A white, killing breath over gardens. He found himself beneath this new vault of frost. It turned into a cold, staring eye studying him:

Jon?[17]

These images of self-examination are extremely important in Vesaas' writing during the 1960's, and also occupy a prominent position among the many images in *The Birds*. Early in that novel Mattis looks in the mirror (to see if he has any gray hairs like Hege has) and catches sight of his own eyes. He tries to look away

> But a pair of eyes pulled him back and wouldn't let go of him.
> He felt like saying to the image in front of him:
> Where in the world did you come from?
> Why did you come?
> He would have received no answer.[18]

Later, when the woodcock is shot Mattis looks into its eyes just as it dies, and it is the thought of these eyes being covered by lids and stones that plagues him during the rest of his life. Another pair of eyes gives Mattis a fright one day he is out in his boat. He has been sitting too long thinking, trying to find the answer to Hege's unhappiness and his part in it, and his old boat has taken in more water than he can bail out:

> Now things happened quickly:
> A pair of eyes appeared in the water and stared straight at him.
> "No!" he shouted.
> His own eyes popped, and the other pair stared back. Nothing but a pair of eyes.
> But he didn't want to.
> "I don't want to!" he shouted, and grew pale.[19]

Mattis is able to row his water-filled boat to a nearby island and save himself, but this scene serves as a forewarning of his later fate.

II   The Ice Palace

Vesaas employs, and broadens the significance of, these same images in the novel *The Ice Palace* (*Is-slottet*, 1963), which followed *The Fire*. *The Ice Palace* tells a very simple story about two little girls who are drawn together by their need for friendship. One of them, Siss, is a happy, extroverted girl with understanding parents and many friends among her schoolmates, for whom she is the leader. The other girl, Unn, is shy and withdrawn. She is new to the village, her unmarried mother having recently died. She lives with her aunt and keeps to herself at school. The two girls take the first steps toward establishing a friendship, and Siss is on the way to visit Unn for the first time at home as the book opens. The opening paragraphs are master-pieces of concentrated mood-setting:

> A young, white forehead boring through the darkness. An eleven-year-old girl. Siss.
> It was really only afternoon, but already dark. A hard frost in late autumn. Stars, but no moon, and no snow to give a glimmer of light—so the darkness was thick, in spite of the stars. On each side was the forest, deathly still, with everything that might be alive and shivering in there at that moment.[20]

The meeting between Siss and Unn is a mixture of boisterous-ness and shyness characteristic of their age. They lock themselves in Unn's room, giggle a little, talk a little about themselves (though mostly about Unn's parents), look at Unn's photo album, have an undressing race, and look into a mirror together:

> Four eyes full of gleams and radiance beneath their lashes, filling the mirror. Questions shooting out and then hiding again. I don't know: Gleams and radiance, gleaming from you to me, from me to you, and from me to you alone—into the mirror and out again, and never an answer about what this is, never an explanation. . . .
> They let the mirror fall, looked at each other with flushed faces, stunned. They shone towards each other, were one with each other; it was an incredible moment.[21]

The contact they feel in this encounter in the mirror helps Unn to begin to open up. She is able to ask Siss a personal question—if Siss had noticed anything unusual about her when they were naked—which reveals that she is confused and perhaps guilt-ridden about her identity, which is not surprising in light of her parentage. Siss is confused and embarrassed by the question, and becomes even more so when Unn tells her she isn't sure that she will go to heaven. But Unn also says that she has something to tell her, although not right then, and this reassures Siss that they will become close friends. The whole meeting is one of hesitation and fumbling and uncertainty, but with a promise, for both of them, that something wonderful will develop from it, though neither of them knows what this might be. As Siss walks home she becomes frightened by everything threatening along the sides of the road, and feels "at the mercy of the unknown."[22]

Unn is even more confused and disturbed by the meeting than Siss, and the next day she feels that it is impossible for her to meet Siss again right away. She decides to stay away from school and instead take a trip along the lake and down the river to a frozen waterfall, a trip that the other children at school had been talking about taking. While walking across the lake she peers down through the clear ice:

It was like looking through a pane of glass.
Just then the sun rose, cold and slanting, and shone through the ice straight down to the brown bottom, with its mud and stones and weeds. . . .
She lay flat on the ice, not yet feeling the cold. Her slim body was a shadow with distorted human form down on the bottom.[23]

Unn slides across the ice, studying the bottom of the lake, and is startled when she suddenly passes the drop-off point and her shadow plunges out of sight. She is even more startled by the sight of something moving toward her:

A fish moving as fast as an arrow, as if making straight for her eyes. She shrank aside, forgetting that there was ice between them. There was a stripe of grey-green back, then a jerk to one side and the flick of a glassy eye to see what she was.
That was all, down again into the depths.[24]

The forewarnings of her fate that are revealed to her in these glimpses are quickly brought to fulfillment. She continues on her way and soon comes to the frozen waterfall: huge and shining like a palace. Unn is enthralled by the sight of it:

It was an enchanted palace. She must try to find a way in![25]

She finds a crack in the ice large enough to squeeze through, and leaves the real world behind. She wanders from one chamber to another, both fascinated and frightened. At one point she thinks:

Why am I here? she thought, as she walked back and forth. Not so many steps, she was walking more and more stiffly and unrecognizably. Why am I here? She attempted to find the solution to this riddle.[26]

Unn finds no answer to the riddle, and squeezes into another, and final, room. Water is dripping from the ceiling and running down the walls of this room, but Unn is now cold and numb and crouches down in a corner to rest. As her thoughts gradually become more and more unclear she suddenly sees something:

There was something in the ice! At first it had no form, but the moment she shouted it took shape, and shone out like an eye of ice up there, confronting her, putting a stop to her thoughts.

It was clearly an eye, a tremendous eye.

It grew wider and wider as it looked at her, from deep in the ice, and full of light.[27]

The winter sun rising above the rim of the valley is Unn's last greeting from the world, and she loses consciousness thinking of the flood of light reaching her trapped in the ice palace.

Unn is, of course, quickly missed. Everyone asks Siss what she knows about Unn's disappearance, but she can, and will, tell them nothing. A search party is formed and they look for Unn along the river and below the waterfall, but find nothing. They, too, feel the enchantment of the ice palace:

The men have to leave, but they do so reluctantly. . . .

They seem possessed, searching feverishly for something precious that has come to grief, yet involved themselves. They are tired, grave men, giving themselves over as sacrifices to an enchantment, saying: It is *here*. They stand at the foot of the ice walls with tense faces, ready to break into a song of mourning before the closed, compelling palace. If one of them had been impetuous enough to begin, all of them would have joined in[28].

Even though all those searching for Unn feel involved in her fate, it is also made clear that this involvement is limited. In the final chapter of the novel the ice palace falls and is swept away when spring has come:

No one can witness the fall of the ice palace. It takes place at night, when all children are asleep.

No one is involved deeply enough to take part in it. A blast of noiseless chaos may cause the air to vibrate in distant bedrooms, but no one wakes up to ask: What is it?[29]

Those who are living must continue to live, and to play their role in life. As obvious as this is, it is difficult for Siss to accept it. She feels that she has a duty to remain true to Unn's memory, and promises herself that she will think of no one but her. During the winter she shuts herself off from contact with those around her. From being a leader among her schoolmates she takes over Unn's role as an outsider, and comes close to retreating into the same state of psychological isolation that drove Unn to her death. For a long time she refuses even to admit the fact of Unn's death, but finally has to. Unn's aunt, whom Siss has felt to be the only other person still thinking about Unn, helps her do this. She has sold her house and plans to move away, an act which Siss takes as a sign that she has given up hope that Unn is alive. She asks Siss to take a walk with her the evening before she leaves. She tells Siss the bitter truth, honestly and directly:

"There's nothing for us to wait for any longer. She's gone and she's not alive."[30]

She also gives Siss the encouragement she needs to return to life:

"Listen, Siss, what I want to ask you before I leave is that you should try to go back to all that you used to have. You said you had made a promise. But it can't come to anything, when the other party to it isn't here any more. You can't bind yourself to her memory, and shut yourself away from what is natural for you."[31]

Siss is still reluctant to believe this, but the words that Unn's aunt says to her take effect on her. This is expressed in a beautiful and evocative image which gives a hint of the change that is about to take place in Siss. When she leaves Unn's aunt to walk home in the darkness, she discovers that there is nothing frightening in the woods bordering the road, as she had felt there was during the dark winter night at the beginning of the novel:

Afraid of the dark? No. Bright woodwind players had appeared and were walking along the sides of the road.[32]

"Woodwind Players" is the title of the third and final section of the novel, and also of the next-to-last chapter, in which the description of Siss's return to life is completed. Shortly after her talk with Unn's aunt Siss suggests to her schoolmates that they all take a trip down the river to see the ice palace once more before it melts. They are amazed at her suggestion, but are thankful for it. The next morning is a bright spring morning, and Siss is excited before the trip:

The excitement of rising sap, the excitement of the scent of damp earth—her heart quivered as she walked among it all. Soft-toned, inciting woodwind players had come, enmeshing Siss in sad and joyful enchantment.[33]

Among her schoolmates there are two in particular to whom Siss is drawn. One of them is the girl who has taken over her old role of leader. When they meet on that spring day, Siss has the sudden thought that they will look into a mirror together, and realizes how the feelings she had experienced in connection with Unn are beginning to repeat themselves. The more mature, heterosexual side of her nature is also beginning to develop, and this is expressed in a fine image involving "the woodwind players" and with overtones of the classical Orpheus legend. After all the children have arrived, they start for the ice palace:

They cut across several small valleys. The sun had become strong and warmed the heather and last year's pale grasses. It smelt like some magic morning when one was quite small, and now it lay like ballast, heavy inside them. All that one did not yet know. There was a little of it in that smell. They moved solemnly, but the low tone of the woodwind players blurred their sight.[34]

As they go through the third, and last, valley contact is established between Siss and a boy toward whom she has begun to feel attracted:

The ground was rough, with thickets and clumps of trees, down in the third valley. They could not help becoming separated as they picked their way forward. The usual brook, brimful of water, was there, with pools and small heads of froth.

Siss found herself alone behind a thicket—and just then someone came alongside. It was the boy who had led the way, now no longer at the head of the procession. She looked into his eyes, and saw that they were brighter than usual. She asked hastily:

"What do you want?"

"I don't quite know," he said.

She felt his eyes on her all the time. He said:

"No one can see us here."

Siss replied:

"No one in the whole world."

"Let's jump across the brook," he said.

He took her hand and they jumped across the brook together. It was strange, and then it was over. He held her little finger for a few

paces after the jump. That was strange too; he noticed that the finger
dug itself into his hand slightly. The finger did so of its own accord.
    They let go quickly, and hurried round the thicket to join the
others.[35]

When they arrive at the ice palace they all clamber out onto it
despite the great danger. Siss tries to warn them, frightened most
by the fact that she has had fantasies of being on the ice palace
when it collapses and being carried away with it, but finally joins
them in scrambling around on it. There is a sudden boom, and
they all, including Siss, react in the same way:

    All of them out on the top turned white and made for dry ground
on two legs or four, whichever was easiest. They had no desire to
ride away with the ice when destruction overtook it; they wanted
to live.
    No no! thought Siss too, as she saved herself.[36]

    The secret of the artistic success of *The Ice Palace* lies in the
combined simplicity of its plot, its style and its imagery. All the
images employed in it are extremely simple images of objects
and events in nature, by means of which Vesaas has nevertheless
succeeded in expressing with great effectiveness the complexities
of adolescent psychological growth and the ever-present struggle
between destructive and life-preserving forces. Many of these
images also appear in earlier books by Vesaas, but the manner in
which they are employed in *The Ice Palace* is somewhat different.
Vesaas frequently, in all of his books from *Children of Man* to
The Ice Palace, intertwines the development of the plot with
lyrical descriptions of images which serve as commentary on or
accompaniment to the plot. These usually take the form of
shorter sections within chapters, of which the passage depicting
the nature of man as an "inner landscape" in *The Seed* (cf. Chapter 4) is a good example. Huskuld's visions and feverish dreams
in *Huskuld the Herald* and Hallstein's dreams and fantasies in
Spring Night can also be taken as examples of such passages. In
the novels that are essentially allegorical or symbolic, such as
The House in Darkness or *The Signal*, such lyrical intermezzi
frequently appear as separate chapters, but this is rare in any of
the novels with a basically realistic plot before *The Ice Palace*.
In this novel, however, several such passages appear as separate
chapters, and have no direct connection with the development of

the plot on the realistic level. Instead, they supplement the realistic plot by depicting Siss's subconscious states of mind.

An example of this is a chapter entitled "The Bird," which is placed in the book after the chapters describing Siss's decision to remain true to Unn's memory. It is a description of how a "wild bird with steel claws,"[37] wheeling through the air above the winter landscape, spots something in the ice palace that makes him dive at it again and again:

He was bound fast here, the prisoner of his own freedom, unable to give up. What he saw confused him.[38]

He is also described as being death, which represents his role in nature as a bird of prey, but this also stands for Siss's fate if she is not able to free herself of the bonds which tie her to the memory of Unn.

A later chapter entitled "A Dream of Snow-covered Bridges" presages the feelings which Siss will later develop for the girl who has taken over as leader, but of which she is unaware during the winter months. The chapter, in its entirety, is set as a poem:

> As we stand the snow falls thicker.
> Your sleeve turns white.
> My sleeve turns white.
> They move between us like
> snow-covered bridges.
>
> But snow-covered bridges are frozen.
> In here is living warmth.
> Your arm is warm beneath the snow, and
> a welcome weight on mine.
>
> It snows and snows
> upon silent bridges.
> Bridges unknown to all.

III   The Bridges

In his next novel, *The Bridges* (*Bruene*, 1966), Vesaas develops this technique still further. In this novel such lyrical intermezzi, standing as separate chapters, appear more frequently than in *The Ice Palace*, and are distributed throughout the novel in such a way that they form a progression of images which parallels the development of the plot on the realistic level.

The plot itself is even simpler than that of *The Ice Palace* and also touches on the problems of illegitimacy, but from a different standpoint, namely that of the mother. Two eighteen-year-olds, Torvil and Aud, have been companions all their lives. Their families assume that they will fall in love, and eventually marry, and they are just at this point in their emotional development when the novel opens. Aud, while walking in the woods behind their houses, discovers the body of a dead baby. She is shocked, and deeply moved, by this discovery, and feels that she and Torvil must protect and support the young mother, whoever she may be, by not telling anyone about it. They later meet the mother, who is a girl of their own age, unmarried and alone in the world. She has herself killed the child and is on the verge of committing suicide. Torvil and Aud continue meeting with her over a period of several days, and the contact with them enables her to regain her faith in life and to reject her plans to destroy herself.

In addition to the many separate chapters which serve as lyrical descriptions of the emotional states of the novel's three characters, there are also, as in all of Vesaas' novels, many other shorter sections within chapters which serve the function of establishing a mood or describing the state of mind of one or more of the characters. The opening paragraphs of the first chapter, for example, set the mood of the entire novel and introduce some of its more important images:

> The wind filtering from the distance; and the old stone bridge over the river, where the high road goes. The dark parapet of the bridge, its stones fretted over time by rain, sun and wind, tall and dominating in the landscape. The mountainside in the one direction does not detract from the bridge and its impressive appearance—daringly built, with wide arches.
>
> A current that looks like still water.
>
> A river that is too deep and powerful for its movements to be visible on this flat valley floor. No rippling of the current against the stones. Great masses of water glide away day and night, and no one thinks about it unless reminded of it. Gliding depths moving past without pause.[39]

Torvil is standing on the bridge, thinking about Aud. He realizes that their relationship is about to change, and that both he and Aud want this change to come about. The image of the bridge is here used to represent a transition from an old state to a new one, and this use of the image is explicit in one of the lyrical chapters later in the novel which depicts Torvil's feelings:

The other side can be glimpsed through thick mist. There are many houses, and a mountain slope.
I walk forward, wanting something. Something new. . . . It is always on the other side.[40]

That the new situation that Torvil is going to as the novel opens is different from what he imagines, is made clear by what happens when he turns to cross the bridge to go home: he is deep in thought and not looking where he is going and is almost struck by a truck. He is shaken by this close call with death, but it is only a prelude to the feeling of shock and horror that is coming when Aud shows him what she has come across in the woods. They have mixed feelings about this discovery. They feel strongly compelled to help the unknown mother, but also cannot help but feel that it would be a relief if the body of the baby were not there the next morning. They decide to return in the morning when it is light and bury the body, and before they leave they cover it with branches and stones, to prevent it from being molested if a dog should happen along. When they return in the morning, the body *is* gone, but they discover that they feel no less involved in the fate of the mother because of this. The key word for them in this situation is *involved*:

Involved. The word did not sound very reassuring. It sounded dangerous and difficult in this situation. They stood and thought about the new position, or whatever it ought to be called, that they now held. They were not two ordinary eighteen-year-olds, they were two involved persons.[41]

The first of the three sections of the novel is entitled "Involved," and this theme occupies as prominent a position in *The Bridges* as it does in *The Fire* and *The Ice Palace*. Aud and Torvil's understandable wish to be allowed to avoid becoming involved in such an unpleasant situation is expressed by an eerie image in a dream Torvil has the night after the discovery of the body of the baby. Torvil's dream is an extension of the situation, and the central figure in it is a dog:

It seemed to climb right out of the parapet and is crossing over slowly, big, long-legged and colourless. The colour is lost in the wisps

of mist billowing round it, and in the yellow-grey gravel on which it
walks. But it is clearly a dog.[42]

In the dream there are two bridges crossing the river:

The old bridge seems to have died many times. It continues to
stand, its stones darkening. The other bridge is not for us. We did
not know it was there until this moment of nightmare.
There seems to be no one there: and yet there is a dog that is
much too big, the sand-coloured dog. Halfway across it meets the
wind that blows eternally on the bridges.
It stands in the wind on the bridges and slowly disintegrates before our eyes. We watch with relief. There is no dog.[43]

This is merely an illusion, however. The dog appears again,
and crosses the bridge. Torvil, as so many other characters in
Vesaas' books, discovers that the demands that life makes must
be faced, unpleasant as they may be. He attempts once more to
deny the presence of the dog, and another dimension is added:

No, I won't do it. It's not mine. If there's a dog loose, then what
of it? It's not mine.
But it's our bridge.[44]

In the course of the remainder of the novel Torvil gradually
learns how "the other bridge" *is* for us, but first he has to finish
the dream, and the second part is more frightening than the first.
The dog crosses the bridge to "his white-rimed plain," and Torvil
finds himself and Aud standing on it:

The circular clearing is framed by dark trees. Tall trees, so that the
land around it is shut out. Not a single bush in the clearing, but the
autumn grass lies rimed and flattened, rimed and glittering under the
enormous moon.[45]

Off at a distance the dog appears. As he moves slowly toward
them, the plain expands and expands, but he comes closer and
closer all the time. When he is near them they see that he has
no eyes. He reaches them, touches Aud with his tongue, and she
disappears. What is most frightening of all to Torvil is that Aud
tells him that she has dreamt that *he* was licked by a blind dog.
This is the state of mind of Torvil and Aud when they meet
Valborg, the mother of the dead baby. She tells them about her-

self and about the state of loneliness and desperation that led her to do what she did. She has herself removed the body, wrapped it and weighted it and sunk it in the river. Her psychological state is depicted in several lyrical intermezzi appearing as separate chapters between the chapters describing the meetings she has with Torvil and Aud. After their first meeting her thoughts keep returning to what is at the bottom of the river:

> Endlessly gliding water—so that every object turned towards it is polished soft and smooth: after an eternity of gliding, stones are as soft as a cheek—while it changes, changes all the time. Sparkling water above hidden forests and hidden chasms—that's how it is in my thoughts.[46]

The subsequent meetings between the three eighteen-year-olds pass without Valborg being helped appreciably, although she feels that just being with Aud and Torvil may somehow give her what she needs. After their second meeting her thoughts have turned to her own fate in an image that is reminiscent of the scene in *The Fire* in which Jon is close to falling into a bottomless pit in a marsh:

> When you feel stripped, and forced to hide. When your feet drag. When the soles of your feet burn. Searching for water, you plunge raving into mud-holes and drag yourself up again laboriously, then look down at yourself trembling. No one must witness this.[47]

Valborg's attitude toward death is ambivalent: although she seeks it, she has nevertheless a strong fear of it:

> Out on the marsh lie tree-trunks and the remains of trees, half submerged. Little by little they will sink silently down.
> Whoever lies in the moss and comes to understand the smell and everything about it, acquires new senses, sharper sight, and can watch the greyish-brown ooze settling. Straight down. . . .
> When you are naked and have acquired new senses; when you have acquired the terror of sinking straight down into the abyss.[48]

After the third meeting with Torvil and Aud Valborg feels even more at a distance from everything that is human, and her state is expressed by a series of images of elemental life of which the first is a disturbing picture of the depths of depression to which a person can be driven by feelings of isolation:

> We are all the creeping things that live along the banks, along the

shores of the river. We fill the nights. We are all the little black
beetles further up on land—we who have small holes to creep into
when the stones above us are turned over. We are all those who bore
in the slime when the current settles. We bore into things and live
for ever. We are down there and in there where the light does not
reach; we have our own light, we crawl past each other with our
lights, and move on, lonely in great darkness.[49]

When she has arrived at this low point Valborg must either
perish, or begin an ascent that will lead her back to life. The impulse which makes it possible for her to take the second course
comes, as so often in Vesaas' writing, through the intercession
of another person. She and Torvil have felt strongly attracted to
each other, but neither has been able to express it clearly. In their
fourth meeting, when Valborg has told them that she feels she
has to leave, Torvil tells her that he and she must remain together.
They agree to meet again the following day, and her changing
mood is depicted in a lyrical chapter in which the negative image
of the abyss is transformed into a positive image of hope and
regeneration:

There is no abyss—even though there was before. There is a well
with rising water in it. The eye is there. It rises as I watch. The water
rises clearly in the well with the image of the new eye shining
within it.[50]

Valborg is now able to see hope even in her reflection in the
river:

Nobody knows who it is standing on the bridge looking down into
the water. And looking to see if the eye from the well is there too.
If it is true it will be here.
Here too.
I won't admit I'm looking for the other. I'm looking for the eye—
and it rises up and *is here*. From deep down it rises up with its
curious light.[51]

Valborg also realizes that she must continue on her own:

I move away trembling.
I leave this place with something in my heart that I cannot name.
All the same I do not feel stripped. I shall not sink straight down.
Instead I can make an effort on my own. It goes through me like
a streak of light that I am to outgrow my condemnation of myself.
The well with rising water. I meet my eye with rising courage.[52]

The next day Valborg tells Torvil that she must leave. It is the thought that she would be taking something from Aud that prompts her, but so does the confidence in herself that she has gained as a result of Torvil's declaration of love. He has difficulty in accepting this, but realizes he must. He is aided in this by the changes that have been taking place within himself during the contact with Valborg and her situation, and these are also expressed in lyrical passages. They are collected in a chapter entitled "The Dog" which introduces the third and final section of the novel. The states of mind which are expressed in these passages are extensions of impressions Torvil has received earlier: impressions of the dog, the icy plain, the bridge, and of the chasm which he has felt growing between Aud and himself. This had its origin in the different ways in which they initially reacted to the discovery of the dead baby, but it has grown wider during the period of their meetings with Valborg. Torvil's feelings about this situation are expressed in a prose poem:

> Here is my groping hand.
> I seem to be *between* the bridges—although no other bridge can be seen. All the same: bridges span *chasms*.
> A hand groping at random. But not anxiously; on the contrary, assured of finding what it seeks. A question that cannot be anything but assured either: Is that you?
> Yes, as you know.[53]

It is not clear here, nor is it necessary that it be, which chasm Torvil is longing to close: that between him and Aud, or that between him and Valborg. Nor is it really important. Torvil, by virtue of the experience in meeting life situations that he is gaining, is learning how to bridge the chasms between himself and other people, and he is aware of the importance of this: "I am at the bridges, I can tell myself; I am there and I belong."[54]

There is a hint at the end of the novel that it is actually the chasm between Torvil and Aud that is being bridged by the experience they are gaining through their contact with Valborg and her problems. When Torvil goes to meet Valborg, Aud goes out walking, across the bridge. After Valborg leaves Torvil, she and Aud meet as they each cross the bridge from different sides:

> They slowed down a little and looked each other in the eye firmly and unafraid. It was a curious moment. Dizzily brief, but curious.

They did not say a word, each gave a slight nod, each was walking as though uplifted by something—and looked the other straight in the eye.

And with that each went across to her own side.

What had happened? Something had happened.

Aud walked faster.[55]

In this final episode of the novel there is also a synthesizing of the three uses of the bridge motif present in Vesaas' writing from *The Tower* on: to represent a transition to a new and unknown state, to depict contact between people, and to stand as a symbol of the eternal. This motif is particularly important in Vesaas' writing in the 1960's. It is the central image of the poem (quoted earlier in this chapter) "A Dream of Snow-covered Bridges" in *The Ice Palace*, and it is also central to one of the most important episodes in *The Fire*. Just before Jon joins the search party looking for the lost girl, he crosses a bridge. This clearly represents a transition to something new and unknown, and at the same time the eternal aspects of the image of the bridge are underlined strongly:

He was aware of the new day, but it was not important out there. There *was* no new day out on the old stone bridge, no night, either— the old stone bridge was outside of time. . . . The movement of the river and the wind cut across the bridge. They had never taken account of time, either, of a lack of days, or too long or too many days.[56]

In *The Bridges* "the wind that blows eternally on the bridges" is present in Torvil's dream about the bridge and the dog (quoted above), and just before Aud meets Valborg at the end of the novel she is standing on the bridge:

It was free and open there in the candid crosswind. Below, in the same channel, the deep current flowed imperceptibly.[57]

As Aud and Valborg cross the bridge swept by the eternal forces of wind and current they are both going to something new and unknown, and their moment of looking into each other's eyes represents a moment of contact and understanding. The bridge motif is thus brought to its culmination in *The Bridges*, where it sets in relief the personal, the social, and the eternal aspects of human existence.

That this same motif figures prominently in *The Fire* and *The Ice Palace* is only one example of the similarities that exist between these three novels. An even more important point of similarity is the experimentation in the balance between plot and imagery present in all of them. This finds expression in *The Fire* in its totally surrealistic form, which makes it difficult to distinguish between the level of plot and the level of imagery, while in *The Ice Palace* and *The Bridges* these two levels are held apart but allowed to develop along parallel lines. In *The Bridges* this technique has been carried so far that the "story" is told simultaneously on the level of imagery and the level of plot. The maturing process which takes place within Valborg, Torvil, and Aud in the course of the novel is described just as completely in the progression of images in the lyrical intermezzi depicting their emotional states as in the accounts of their meetings and conversations. The lyrical passages are so intense and forceful, in fact, that they tend to overshadow the more realistic sections of the novel, and the result is that the level of plot serves as scarcely more than a scaffolding for the level of imagery.

IV   The Boat of Evening

That this period of experimentation in Vesaas' writing is not over is clearly indicated by the form of his most recent book, *The Boat of Evening* (*Båten om kvelden,* 1968). In this book the scaffolding of realistic plot has been in effect removed, and the reader is confronted with little more than a series of images described in highly lyrical language. The result is a book which makes the greatest possible demands on the reader's ability to make associations. He is provided with something of an aid to interpretation in the fact that two of the chapters are clearly autobiographical, and describe various facets of Vesaas' relationships to his parents during his childhood and youth. Several other chapters appear to contain a great deal of autobiographical material, but it would be a mistake to assume that everything in the book is to be taken as directly depicting events in Vesaas' own life. A clear indication of this is a chapter entitled "A Morning with Shining Horses" which describes an experience shared by two adolescent boys whose relationship is reminiscent of that

between Per Bufast and Olav Bringa in *The Great Cycle.* One of
the boys in this chapter is even named Per, while the other—the
narrator who refers to himself in the first person—is unnamed. But
Vesaas has specifically stated that he had no such friend during
his adolescence ("But Olav Bringa never existed—he's pure fic-
tion beginning to end."[58]), and it is thus clear that at least this
chapter contains a certain amount of fictional material.

Even though it would be neither possible nor necessarily fruit-
ful to try to connect the contents of all the chapters in *The Boat
of Evening* with specific events in Vesaas' life, it is clear that they
are all reflections of his feelings about and experience of life, in
the same sense that the images and events in all his writings are.
There are also, quite naturally, very close connections between
the imagery in *The Boat of Evening* and the imagery in the rest
of his writing. The imagery of this book is so inclusive, as a matter of fact, that the plots of all his novels and stories function in
a very real sense as the level of plot which has been omitted here.
The main disadvantage of such an interpretation of this book,
however, would be that it would place unnecessary restrictions
on the reader, who should feel free to make any associations he
feels inclined to on the basis of the images presented to him.

The reader is aided in this by the nature of the language in the
book, which is highly lyrical and evocative. In everything he has
written Vesaas has balanced delicately on the borderline between
prose and poetry, and it has often been difficult to distinguish
between these two uses of language in his work. In *The Boat of
Evening* the distinction between prose and poetry has been for all
practical purposes eliminated. The first section of the book is in
the form of two prefaces: the first consisting of two poems, the
second of one poem. The final section of the book is formally its
final chapter and is set as prose, but it is no less lyrical than the
poems of the prefaces and the decision to set it as prose seems to
have been an arbitrary one. This applies as well to many of the
chapters which make up the bulk of the book, and in several of
them there is an alternation between prose and poetic sections
that is indicative of the intensely lyrical nature of their language.

The highly lyrical nature of *The Boat of Evening* is not surprising in light of the fact that its title and its central image are
derived from a poem which appeared in *The Land of Hidden
Fires* in 1953:

THE BOAT ON SHORE

Your quiet boat
is nameless.
Your quiet boat
is harborless.
Your hidden boat on shore.

For this is no harbor
The leaves glisten palely on spring nights
above the waiting, ready boat,
and sift yellow and wet
onto its thwarts in October,
and no one has been here.

But there is a pulling here from endless
plains of sea,
where suns rise up from the depths
and the wind blows toward the harbor beyond.

But that is no harbor either,
but only a place filled with pulling and calling
from still wider plains,
more violent storms along the shores,
and a still larger boat in the evening.

Your quiet boat
is slowly being overgrown.
Your hidden boat on shore.

The centrality of water imagery in *The Boat of Evening* is evident from the content of the first poem of the first preface:

My first dream
My fine dream
about gliding water and my dream.

The heart dwells beside flowing rivers.
The rivers eat away the shores as they pass.
Narrowing shores lose their names.

There are always shores
for a dream
about gliding water and my dream.

The images of these poems are developed in several chapters in the books, especially in a chapter toward the end entitled "The

Heart Lies Naked Beside the Great Highway in the Darkness,"
which is a dream about "distant shores ... and unknown har-
bors,"[59] and about the storm which will drive the boat toward
them when the time comes.

It is not only the images of the boat, the storm, and the great
expanses of water that connect the imagery of *The Boat of Evening*
with that of the poem "The Boat on Shore," but also the concept
of wasted opportunities. In the poem the boat, though waiting
and ready, is never used and becomes gradually overgrown. This
same idea is expressed in several different ways in *The Boat of
Evening*. The second poem of the first preface, which was published in a slightly different form in 1965[60] begins:

> That waiting for the snake,
> the child standing, waiting in fear
> for the snake to come out.
>
> Nothing appeared,
> year after year.
> Nothing slithered out beneath a heel.

This feeling of time passing and nothing being accomplished is
also expressed, partially through the use of the same image, in the
only other section of the book to have been published earlier,[61]
namely, the chapter entitled "The Wasted Day Crawls off on Its
Belly":

> No one talks about the wasted day.
> The wasted day crawls off on its belly.
> Only the chairs are left standing stiffly in place, in the lecture halls.
> Our empty chairs in the lecture halls—because the day is over.
> The day which was no day, is over. We nodded wisely, and went
> home. It turned out to be a day of shame and will never show itself
> again. Nothing is nothing, the day is past, it is evening and the wind
> rises.[62]

The empty chairs are filled during the night by "the wise heads
from the graves,"[63] who debate "the eternal case of the Butcher's
Shop of Sirius," expressed in a poem which fills the central section of the chapter, and which contains a frequently repeated
line identical with the attempt made by Torvil in *The Bridges*
to rid himself of the thought of the unpleasant situation he doesn't
wish to face: "There is no dog."

An indication of what sort of situation gave rise to the images of shame and frustration in this chapter is to be found in the chapter which immediately follows it: "Washed Cheeks." This chapter describes, in a beautiful prose poem, five dead soldiers in a peaceful grove of trees, their faces washed by the rain, shining in the darkness of the night.

Several chapters provide insights into various aspects of the problem of contact and communication. A chapter entitled "In the Marshes and on the Earth" sheds a great deal of light on the feelings of Mattis in *The Birds* during his period of communication with the woodcock. Vesaas describes the dancing of cranes in a marsh early one morning:

> Within my numb body there is a commotion in time with the dancing of the cranes. Their dancing has reached me. I cannot see the little pools like eyes in the marsh, but I know how they glisten indifferently. My own are burning. It is all both tormenting and exciting. It is tormenting to have to stand so much. You have to take part as best you can in the suppressed rhythm of the wild dance of the cranes. If only you could take part with movements and with shouts. Trumpet with the trumpeting birds about all there is to be known.[64]

This feeling of identification with the cranes grows stronger when two of them approach and their eyes meet those of the boy lying in the marsh:

> They are not afraid, but they are careful to have enough room to open their wings if they should have to. Do they have an open line to me, I wonder. I wish they did. An open path, along which we can look for everything incomprehensible we have in common, while we wander through the marshes and on the earth.[65]

The deep lyrical strain present in this description of a young boy's experience also appears in calmer, but no less intense, form in a short prose chapter near the end of the book. The utter simplicity of the situation and the language used to express it is caught in the first sentences:

> Seems to be such a small thing.
> It doesn't take much.
> Just walking up and fetching the milk pail early in the morning can be a miracle.[66]

The description of this everyday situation at Midtbö or any other home in the country extends over only three short pages but in it Vesaas is nevertheless able to capture, in a series of evocative images, the beauty and meaning of existence. At the end of the description he sums up the significance of these images for him at his present stage of life:

Flowers among the stones, and nearly fully developed buds. The sun will pour down and the odors change as everything is brought to life. You can already see it: there has never been such wild blossoming on the hills as this year. As there will be, since many of the flowers are not open yet. You are part of this. Belong here.

The overwhelming feeling of being a part of something. In wonderment you walk up the hill, bathed in everything that is strange, just to fetch the milk pail.[67]

This feeling of being a part of something, and being where one belongs, such as is experienced by so many of Vesaas' more fortunate characters—among others, Knut in the short story "Last Man Home," Per Bufast, even Klas Dyregodt and Jon in *The Fire* at the end of their long and arduous developments—is also expressed in *The Boat of Evening* through the use of its central image of water. In the final chapter, entitled "The Rivers Beneath the Earth," the significance of the image is deepened and extended:

Both night and day.
You are alone and feel this: Isn't the ground trembling beneath your feet, because of rivers hidden somewhere?
And what is there to do?
You have to be present.
You have to appear, and stand in the flow of water. You have to let the tiny trembling shake you. Like half-decayed bridges tremble slightly when the rivers are filled with water from the melting snow.[68]

For the person who has found his place within the flow of not only life, but the totality of existence, the coming of night holds no fear. This is expressed in a final image which sums up, and extends beyond the borders of life itself, the state of self-awareness and openness so central to all of Vesaas' writing:

This is the way night *is*. Different, but not unfriendly. The currents flow swiftly back.
What then?
It is all right.
The night opens its clear vault, and your own eye opens its. All eyes are large in the night, and opened wide. They are dark out to their edges.[69]

Notes and References

Chapter One

1. *Vindane* (Oslo, 1952) p. 102.
2. *Ibid.*, pp. 105–07.
3. *Leiret og hjulet* (Oslo, 1936) p. 91.
4. *Ibid.*, pp. 100–02.
5. Stig Dagerman, "Ett barns memoarer," *Vårt behov av tröst* (Stockholm, 1955).
6. *Leiret og hjulet*, p. 12.
7. *Vårnatt* (Oslo, 1954) pp. 20–21; *The Seed/Spring Night*. Tr. by Kenneth G. Chapman (Oslo, 1964) p. 162.
8. *Vårnatt*, p. 22; *Spring Night*, p. 163.
9. "Om skrivaren," *Ei bok om Tarjei Vesaas* (Oslo, 1964) p. 29.
10. *Grindegard* (Oslo, 1925) p. 80.
11. *Ibid.*, p. 81.
12. *Klokka i haugen* (Oslo, 1929) p. 60.
13. *Sendemann Huskuld* (Oslo, 1924) pp. 184–185.
14. *Ibid.*, p. 245.
15. *Ibid.*, p. 246–47.
16. *Ibid.*, p. 248.
17. *Ibid.*, p. 249.

Chapter Two

1. "Poesi—og tronge tider," *Fritt ord*, 1939; reprinted in *Tarjei Vesaas* (Oslo, 1964) p. 51.
2. "Om skrivaren," *Ei bok om Tarjei Vesaas.* (Oslo, 1964) p. 22.
3. *Ibid.*, p. 19.
4. *Grindegard* (Oslo, 1925) p. 7.
5. *Ibid.*, p. 136.
6. *Sendemann Huskuld* (Oslo, 1924) p. 72.
7. *Menneskebonn* (Oslo, 1923) p. 23.
8. Ragnvald Skrede, *Tarjei Vesaas* (Oslo, 1947) p. 18; "Om skrivaren," p. 13.
9. *Menneskebonn*, p. 24.
10. *Ibid.*, p. 55.
11. *Ibid.*, p. 84.
12. *Grindegard*, p. 155.
13. *Ibid.*, p. 159.
14. *Ibid.*, p. 201.
15. *Guds bustader* (Oslo, 1925) p. 69.

16. *Menneskebonn*, p. 5.
17. *Ibid.*, p. 101.
18. *Ibid.*, p. 38.
19. *Ibid.*, p. 87.
20. *Ibid.*, pp. 90–91.
21. *Ibid.*, p. 111.
22. Harald Naess, "Et forsök over Vesaas' prosastil," *Edda*, 1962, p. 160.
23. *Sendemann Huskuld*, p. 7.
24. *Ibid.*, p. 218.
25. *Ibid.*, p. 252.
26. "Om skrivaren," pp. 15–17.
27. Naess, *op. cit.*, pp. 167–68.
28. "Til mi solmöy," *Jolehögtid* (Oslo, 1921).
29. "Blomar yver land," *Syn og Segn* (Oslo, 1922) pp. 283–84.
30. *Sendemann Huskuld*, pp. 189–90.
31. *Grindegard*, p. 9.
32. *Ibid.*, p. 13.
33. *Ibid.*, p. 14.
34. *Grindekveld* (Oslo, 1926) p. 109.
35. *Grindekveld, loc cit.*
36. *Ibid.*, p. 140.
37. *Ibid.*, p. 142.
38. *Ibid.*, p. 141.

Chapter Three

1. *Dei svarte hestane* (Oslo, 1928) p. 27.
2. *Ibid.*, p. 341.
3. *Ibid.*, p. 25.
4. *Die Glocke im Hügel*. Erzählungen aus den norwegischen Bergland. Ins Deutsche übertragen von Helen Uhlschmid-Woditzka (Graz, 1934).
5. *Klokka i haugen* (Oslo, 1929) p. 79.
6. *Ibid.*, p. 80.
7. *Ibid.*, p. 81.
8. *Ibid.*, pp. 83–84.
9. *Fars reise* (Oslo, 1930) p. 22.
10. *Ibid.*, p. 23.
11. *Ibid.*, p. 34.
12. *Ibid.*, p. 35.
13. *Ibid.*, p. 220.
14. *Ibid.*, p. 27.
15. *Sigrid Stallbrokk* (Oslo, 1931) p. 58.
16. *Ibid.*, p. 131.

17. *Dei ukjende mennene* (Oslo, 1932) p. 95.
18. *Ibid.*, p. 96.
19. *Ibid.*, p. 97.
20. *Ibid.*, p. 100.
21. *Ibid.*, p. 156.
22. *Ibid.*, p. 171.
23. *Ibid.*, p. 173.
24. "Om skrivaren," pp. 14–15.
25. "Gift i blodet," *Den 17. mai,* March 31, 1926.
26. Skrede, *op. cit.*, p. 107.
27. "Vakt ved Rhinen," *Den 17. mai,* October 7, 1932.
28. *Uultimatum* (Oslo, 1934) p. 96.
29. *Ibid.*, p. 7.
30. "Om skrivaren," p. 25.
31. *Kjeldene* (Oslo, 1946) pp. 32–33.
32. *Sandeltreet* (Oslo, 1933) p. 125.
33. *Ibid.*, p. 50.
34. *Ibid.*, p. 81.
35. *Ibid.*, p. 37.
36. *Ibid.*, p. 39.
37. *Ibid.*, p. 89.
38. *Ibid.*, p. 119.
39. *Ibid.*, p. 120.
40. *Ver ny, vår draum* (Oslo, 1956) pp. 73–75.
41. *Sandeltreet*, p. 71.
42. *Ibid.*, p. 159.
43. *Ibid.*, pp. 170–71.
44. *Det store spelet* (Oslo, 1934) pp. 23–24; *The Great Cycle.*
Tr. by Elizabeth Rokkan. (Madison, 1967) p. 18.
45. *Det store spelet*, p. 59; *The Great Cycle*, p. 44.
46. *Det store spelet*, p. 284; *The Great Cycle*, p. 211.
47. *Det store spelet*, p. 296; *The Great Cycle*, p. 218.
48. *Det store spelet*, pp. 298–99; *The Great Cycle*, p. 221.
49. *Det store spelet*, p. 300; *The Great Cycle*, p. 222.
50. *Det store spelet*, p. 301; *The Great Cycle*, p. 223.
51. *Det store spelet*, p. 120; *The Great Cycle*, p. 88.
52. "Om skrivaren," p. 26.
53. *Kvinnor ropar heim* (Oslo, 1935) pp. 284–85.
54. *Ibid.*, p. 26.
55. *Ibid.*, p. 176.
56. *Ibid.*, p. 116.
57. *Ibid.*, p. 391.
58. *Leiret og hjulet* (Oslo, 1936) p. 151.
59. *Ibid.*, p. 106.
60. *Ibid.*, p. 120.

61. "Om skrivaren," p. 26.
62. *Hjarta höyrer sine heimlandstonar* (Oslo, 1938) pp. 39–40.
63. *Ibid.*, p. 16.
64. *Ibid.*, p. 209.
65. *Ibid.*, p. 311.
66. *Det store spelet*, p. 129; *The Great Cycle*, p. 95.
67. *Hjarta höyrer sine heimlandstonar*, p. 195.
68. *Ibid.*, pp. 15–16.
69. *Ibid.*, p. 13.
70. Skrede, *op. cit.*, p. 147; "Forord," *Kimen* (Oslo, 1967) p. 5.
71. "Poesi—og tronge tider," *Fritt ord*, 1939; reprinted in *Tarjei Vesaas* (Oslo, 1964) pp. 49–50.

Chapter Four

1. "Forord," *Kimen* (Oslo, 1967) p. 5.
2. *Kimen* (Oslo, 1958) p. 130; *The Seed/Spring Night*. Tr. by Kenneth G. Chapman (Oslo, 1964) p. 88.
3. *Kimen*, p. 198; *The Seed*, p. 136.
4. *Kimen*, p. 8; *The Seed*, p. 4.
5. *Kimen*, p. 43; *The Seed*, p. 26.
6. *Kimen*, p. 44; *The Seed*, pp. 26–27.
7. *Kimen*, p. 96; *The Seed*, p. 64.
8. *Kimen*, p. 109–10; *The Seed*, pp. 73–74.
9. *Kimen*, p. 211–12; *The Seed*, pp. 146–47.
10. *Kimen*, p. 209; *The Seed*, p. 144.
11. *Kimen*, p. 159; *The Seed*, p. 108.
12. *Kimen*, p. 204; *The Seed*, p. 140.
13. *Kimen*, p. 34; *The Seed*, p. 22.
14. "Forord," *Kimen*, *loc. cit.*
15. Skrede, *op. cit.*, p. 147.
16. *Bleikeplassen* (Oslo, 1946) p. 5.
17. *Ibid.*, p. 6.
18. *Ibid.*, p. 8.
19. *Ibid.*, p. 10.
20. *Ibid.*, p. 5.
21. *Ibid.*, p. 13.
22. *Ibid.*, p. 24.
23. *Ibid.*, p. 164.
24. *Ibid.*, p. 76.
25. *Ibid.*, p. 214.
26. *Ibid.*, p. 221.
27. *Tårnet* (Oslo, 1948) p. 14.

28. *Ibid.*, p. 9.
29. *Ibid.*, p. 24.
30. *Ibid.*, p. 288.
31. *Ibid.*, p. 289.
32. *Ibid.*, p. 279.
33. "Regnbågen över snön," *Vårt behov av tröst* (Stockholm, 1955) p. 278.
34. *Grindegard*, p. 113.
35. *Tårnet*, p. 34.
36. *Ibid.*, p. 169.
37. *Ibid.*, p. 61.
38. *Ibid.*, p. 39.
39. *Ibid.*, p. 266.
40. *Huset i mörkret* (Oslo, 1945) p. 7.
41. *Ibid.*, p. 23.
42. *Ibid.*, pp 144–45.
43. *Ibid.*, p. 330.
44. *Ibid.*, p. 334.
45. *Ibid.*, p. 339.
46. *Signalet* (Oslo, 1950) p. 148.
47. *Ibid.*, p. 234.
48. *Kimen*, p. 181.
49. *Huset i mörkret*, p. 218.
50. *Signalet*, p. 8.
51. Cf. Robert Jay Lifton, *Death in Life: Survivors of Hiroshima* (New York, 1968).
52. "Om skrivaren," p. 15.
53. *Signalet*, pp. 81–82.
54. *Ibid.*, p. 147.
55. "Reisedraumen," *Juleglede* (Oslo, 1949) pp. 16–18.
56. "Ved tunnel-gapet," *Teknisk ukeblad* (Oslo, 1958); reprinted in *Tarjei Vesaas* (Oslo, 1964) p. 68.

Chapter Five

1. E.g., "Mot skiftet," *For bygd og by* (Oslo, 1923) No. 4, p. 60; "Heilage jord," *Urd* (Oslo, 1924) p. 535.
2. "Fonnine," *Urd* (Oslo, 1925) p. 179; cf. *Dei svarte hestane*, p. 327.
3. *Grindegard*, p. 118.
4. *Guds bustader*, p. 40.
5. *Menneskebonn*, pp. 11–13.
6. *Kimen*, p. 58; *The Seed/Spring Night*, p. 37.
7. *Fars reise*, p. 116.

8. *Sigrid Stallbrokk*, p. 142.
9. *Sandeltreet*, p. 170.
10. *Det store spelet*, p. 211; *The Great Cycle*, p. 158.
11. "Om skrivaren," pp. 25, 27.
12. *Ibid.*, p. 32.

Chapter Six

1. "Kornet over havet," *Norsk ukeblad*, No. 19, 1942 (Oslo) pp. 6–8, 21.
2. "Naken," *Kvinnen og tiden*, No. 2, 1946 (Oslo) pp. 12–13.
3. "Poesi—og tronge tider," *Fritt ord*. Utgitt av Nansenskolen, 1939; reprinted in *Tarjei Vesaas* (Oslo, 1964) p. 55.
4. *Leiret og hjulet*, p. 136.
5. *Ibid.*, p. 152.
6. *Ibid.*, p. 174.
7. *Vindane* (Oslo, 1952) p. 144.
8. *Ibid.*, p. 148.
9. *Ibid.*, p. 154.
10. *Ibid.*, pp. 155–56.
11. *Ibid.*, p. 159.
12. *Ibid.*, p. 161.
13. *Loc. cit.*
14. "Vesle-Trask," *Syn og Segn*, 1947, pp. 281–88.
15. *Vindane*, p. 87.
16. *Ibid.*, p. 92.
17. *Ibid.*, pp. 97–98.
18. *Ibid.*, pp. 64–65.
19. *Ein vakker dag* (Oslo, 1959) p. 29.
20. *Ibid.*, pp. 29–30.
21. *Ibid.*, p. 32.
22. *Ibid.*, pp. 39–40.
23. *Vindane*, p. 40.
24. "Kraft," *Julehelg* (Oslo, 1946) pp. 20–22.
25. *Vindane*, p. 43.
26. *Ibid.*, p. 59.
27. *Ein vakker dag*, p. 113.
28. *Ibid.*, p. 120. Tr. by James W. Brown.
29. *Ibid.*, p. 121. Tr. by James W. Brown.
30. First published in *Magasinet For Alle*, No. 23, 1939 (Oslo) pp. 14–18, 34.
31. *Vindane*, pp. 8–9. Tr. by Tim Schiff.
32. *Ibid.*, p. 14. Tr. by Tim Schiff.
33. *Ibid.*, p. 16. Tr. by Tim Schiff.

34. *Ein vakker dag*, p. 195. Tr. by Tim Schiff in *The American-Scandinavian Review*, LVI, 287.

35. *Ibid.*, p. 196. Tr. by Tim Schiff in *The American-Scandinavian Review*, LVI, 287.

36. *Ibid.*, p. 202. Tr. by Tim Schiff in *The American-Scandinavian Review*, LVI, 290.

37. *Ibid.*, p. 203. Tr. by Tim Schiff in *The American-Scandinavian Review*, LVI, 290.

38. *Ibid.*, p. 76.

39. "Fjernstyrt teater," *Vinduet* (Oslo, 1952) pp. 167–68.

40. *Loc. cit.*

41. *Vårnatt.* (Oslo, 1954) p. 19; *The Seed/Spring Night.* Tr. by Kenneth G. Chapman, Universitetsforlaget (Oslo, 1964) p. 161. In the English edition the name Hallstein has been changed to Olaf.

42. *Vårnatt*, p. 29; *Spring Night*, pp. 168–69.

43. *Vårnatt*, p. 32; *Spring Night*, p. 170.

44. *Vårnatt*, pp. 32–33; *Spring Night*, pp. 171–72.

45. *Vårnatt*, p. 35; *Spring Night*, p. 173.

46. *Vårnatt*, p. 54; *Spring Night*, p. 186.

47. *Vårnatt*, p. 51; *Spring Night*, p. 184.

48. *Vårnatt*, p. 132; *Spring Night*, pp. 243–44.

49. *Vårnatt*, pp. 145–46; *Spring Night*, p. 253.

50. *Vårnatt*, pp. 195–96; *Spring Night*, pp. 289–90.

51. *Vårnatt*, p. 196; *Spring Night*, p. 290.

52. *Vårnatt*, p. 227; *Spring Night*, p. 313.

53. "Om Tusten," *Impuls*, No. 2, 1959 (Oslo); reprinted in *Tarjei Vesaas* (Oslo, 1964) p. 72.

54. *Vindane*, p. 229. Tr. by Mary Jennings.

55. *Ibid.*, p. 232. Tr. by Mary Jennings.

56. *Ibid.*, pp. 244–45. Tr. by Mary Jennings.

57. *Ibid.*, p. 246. Tr. by Mary Jennings.

58. *Fuglane* (Oslo, 1957) p. 12; *The Birds.* Tr. by T. Stöverud and M. Barnes (London, 1968) pp. 9–10.

59. *Fuglane*, p. 13; *The Birds*, pp. 10–11.

60. *Fuglane*, p. 26; *The Birds*, p. 22.

61. *Fuglane*, p. 27; *The Birds*, pp. 22–23.

62. *Fuglane*, p. 30; *The Birds*, p. 25.

63. *Fuglane*, p. 85; *The Birds*, pp. 75–76.

64. *Fuglane*, p. 86; *The Birds*, p. 77.

65. *Fuglane*, p. 183; *The Birds*, p. 168.

66. *Fuglane*, pp. 243–44; *The Birds*, p. 224.

Chapter Seven

1. *Ein vakker dag,* p. 213.
2. *Ibid.,* p. 214.
3. *Ibid.,* p. 216.
4. *Brannen* (Oslo, 1961) p. 10.
5. *Ibid.,* pp. 6–7.
6. *Ibid.,* p. 183.
7. *Ibid.,* p. 16.
8. *Ibid.,* p. 22.
9. *Ibid.,* p. 21.
10. *Ibid.,* p. 128.
11. *Ibid.,* p. 133.
12. *Ibid.,* pp. 80–81.
13. *Ibid.,* p. 189.
14. *Ibid.,* p. 196.
15. *Ibid.,* pp. 208–209.
16. *Ibid.,* p. 187.
17. *Ibid.,* p. 183.
18. *Fuglane,* p. 19; *The Birds,* p. 16.
19. *Fuglane,* p. 112; *The Birds,* p. 101.
20. *Is-slottet* (Oslo, 1963) p. 7; *The Ice Palace.* Tr. by Elizabeth Rokkan (London, 1966) p. 7. The American edition is called *The Palace of Ice* (New York, 1968).
21. *Is-slottet,* p. 25; *The Ice Palace,* p. 23.
22. *Is-slottet,* p. 38; *The Ice Palace,* p. 32.
23. *Is-slottet,* pp. 49–50; *The Ice Palace,* pp. 42–43.
24. *Is-slottet,* p. 51; *The Ice Palace,* p. 44.
25. *Is-slottet,* p. 57; *The Ice Palace,* p. 49.
26. *Is-slottet,* p. 64; *The Ice Palace,* p. 54.
27. *Is-slottet,* p. 68; *The Ice Palace,* pp. 57–58.
28. *Is-slottet,* p. 103; *The Ice Palace,* p. 87.
29. *Is-slottet,* p. 206; *The Ice Palace,* p. 175.
30. *Is-slottet,* p. 167; *The Ice Palace,* p. 141.
31. *Is-slottet,* p. 167; *The Ice Palace,* pp. 141–42.
32. *Is-slottet,* p. 170; *The Ice Palace,* p. 144.
33. *Is-slottet,* p. 189; *The Ice Palace,* pp. 160–61.
34. *Is-slottet,* p. 196; *The Ice Palace,* p. 166.
35. *Is-slottet,* pp. 199–200; *The Ice Palace,* pp. 169–70.
36. *Is-slottet,* pp. 202–203; *The Ice Palace,* p. 172.
37. *Is-slottet,* p. 131; *The Ice Palace,* p. 111.
38. *Is-slottet,* p. 133; *The Ice Palace,* p. 112.
39. *Bruene* (Oslo, 1966) p. 7; *The Bridges.* Tr. by Elizabeth Rokkan (London, 1969) p. 9.
40. *Bruene,* pp. 134–35; *The Bridges,* p. 112.

41. *Bruene*, pp. 65–66; *The Bridges*, p. 55.
42. *Bruene*, p. 44; *The Bridges*, p. 38.
43. *Bruene*, pp. 44–45; *The Bridges*, p. 39.
44. *Bruene*, p. 45; *The Bridges*, p. 40.
45. *Bruene*, p. 46; *The Bridges*, p. 40.
46. *Bruene*, p. 123; *The Bridges*, pp. 102–103.
47. *Bruene*, p. 153; *The Bridges*, p. 127.
48. *Bruene*, p. 154; *The Bridges*, pp. 127–28.
49. *Bruene*, p. 173; *The Bridges*, p. 143.
50. *Bruene*, p. 201; *The Bridges*, p. 163.
51. *Bruene*, pp. 201–202; *The Bridges*, p. 164.
52. *Bruene*, p. 202; *The Bridges*, p. 165.
53. *Bruene*, pp. 135–36; *The Bridges*, p. 113.
54. *Bruene*, p. 135; *The Bridges*, p. 113.
55. *Bruene*, p. 225; *The Bridges*, p. 183.
56. *Brannen*, pp. 154–55.
57. *Bruene*, p. 223; *The Bridges*, p. 182.
58. "Om skivaren," p. 12.
59. *Båten om kvelden* (Oslo, 1968) p. 156.
60. "Ormen i Ormekrå." *Dagbladet*, Oslo, January 23, 1965.
61. "Den forspilte dagen kryp bort på buken." *Aftenposten*, Oslo, August 19, 1967.
62. *Båten om kvelden*, p. 103.
63. *Ibid.*, p. 106.
64. *Ibid.*, p. 42.
65. *Ibid.*, p. 48.
66. *Ibid.*, p. 177.
67. *Ibid.*, pp. 179–80.
68. *Ibid.*, p. 207.
69. *Ibid.*, p. 209.

Selected Bibliography

A. ENGLISH TRANSLATIONS OF WORKS BY TARJEI VESAAS

1. Novels (in the order of their original publication in Norwegian)

The Great Cycle. Tr. by Elizabeth Rokkan with an Introduction by Harald S. Naess. The University of Wisconsin Press. Madison. 1967. (*Det store spelet*, 1934.)

The Seed and *Spring Night*. Tr. by Kenneth G. Chapman. The American-Scandinavian Foundation. New York./Universitetsforlaget. Oslo. 1964. (*Kimen*, 1940; *Vårnatt*, 1954.)
(*The Seed*. British Commonwealth Edition. Peter Owen. London. 1966.)

The Birds. Tr. by Torbjörn Stöverud and Michael Barnes. Peter Owen. London. 1968. (*Fuglane*, 1957.)

The Ice Palace. Tr. by Elizabeth Rokkan. Peter Owen. London. 1966. (*Is-slottet*, 1963.)
(*The Palace of Ice*. American Edition. William Morrow and Co. New York. 1968.)

The Bridges. Tr. by Elizabeth Rokkan. Peter Owen. London. 1969. (*Bruene*, 1966.)

2. Short Stories (in the order of the original publication in Norwegian)

"Never Tell It." Tr. by Kenneth G. Chapman. *The American-Scandinavian Review*, Vol. XLVII, No. 2, pp. 166–71. New York. 1959. ("Aldri fortelje det" from *Leiret og hjulet*, 1936.)

"Twenty-one." Tr. by Kenneth G. Chapman. *New World Writing*, No. 14, pp. 269–80. New American Library. New York. 1958. ("21 år" from *Leiret og hjulet*, 1936.)

"In the Fish's Golden Youth." Tr. by Tim Schiff. *The American-Scandinavian Review*, Vol. LVI, No. 3, pp. 287–90. New York. 1968. ("I fiskens grönne ungdom" from *Ein vakker dag*, 1959.)

"Snow." Tr. by Kenneth G. Chapman. *The Literary Review*, Vol. 12, No. 2, pp. 170–75. Teaneck. 1969. ("Det snör og snör" from *Ein vakker dag*, 1959.)

3. Poems (in the order of their original publication in Norwegian)

"Snow and Fir Forests." Tr. by Martin and Inga Allwood. *Twentieth century Scandinavian Poetry*. Pp. 170–71. Oslo. 1950. ("Snö og granskog" from *Kjeldene*, 1946.)

176

"Once Upon a Time." Tr. by Martin and Inga Allwood. *Twentieth Century Scandinavian Poetry.* Pp. 171–72. Oslo. 1950. ("Det var eingong . . ." from *Leiken og lynet,* 1947.)

"In Deep Liability." Tr. by Robert Bly. *The Literary Review,* Vol. 12, No. 2, 1969. p. 222. Teaneck. ("I ansvars naud" from *Leiken og lynet,* 1947.)

"Rain in Hiroshima." Tr. by James W. Brown. *The Literary Review,* Vol. 12, No. 2, pp. 220–21. Teaneck. 1969. ("Regn i Hiroshima" from *Leiken og lynet,* 1947.)

"One Rows and Rows." Tr. James W. Brown. *The Literary Review,* Vol. 12, No. 2, pp. 218–19. Teaneck. 1969. ("Det ror og ror" from *Lykka for ferdesmenn,* 1949.)

"Your Knees and Mine." Tr. James W. Brown. *The Literary Review,* Vol. 12, No. 2, p. 217. Teaneck. 1969. ("Dine knaer og mine" from *Ver ny, vår draum,* 1956.)

B. ARTICLES IN ENGLISH ABOUT TARJEI VESAAS

BEYER, EDWARD. "Tarjei Vesaas." *Scandinavica,* Vol. 3, No. 2, pp. 97–109. London. 1964.

DALE, JOHANNES. "Tarjei Vesaas." *The American-Scandinavian Review,* Vol. LIV, No. 4, pp. 369–74. New York. 1966.

McFARLANE, JAMES W. "Tarjei Vesaas." In *Ibsen and the Temper of Norwegian Literature.* Pp. 182–87. Oxford University Press. 1960.

C. BOOKS AND ARTICLES IN THE SCANDINAVIAN LANGUAGES ABOUT TARJEI VESAAS

SKREDE, RAGNVALD. *Tarjei Vesaas.* Glydendal Norsk Forlag. Oslo. 1947.

Tarjei Vesaas. Serprent av 50-års heftet i *Syn og Segn.* Det norske samlaget. Oslo. 1947.

Tarjei Vesaas. Et skrift lagt fram på Kulturutvalgets Tarjei Vesaas-aften. Red. av Jan Erik Vold. Utg. av Kulturutvalget i Det norske Studentersamfund. Oslo. 1964.

Ei bok om Tarjei Vesaas. Av ti nordiske studentar. Ved Leif Maehle. Det norske samlaget. Oslo. 1964.

Tarjei Vesaas. Festskrift på 70-års dagen. Gyldendal Norsk Forlag. Oslo. 1967.

BROSTROM, TORBEN. "Tarjei Vesaas' symbolverden belyst ud fra hans prosaverker 1940–50." *Edda.* Pp. 28–105. Oslo. 1955.

DAGERMAN, STIG. "Regnbågen över snön." *Vårt behov av tröst.* Pp. 277–80. Norstedts. Stockholm. 1955. (Reprinted in *Tarjei Vesaas.* Et skrift lagt fram på Kulturutvalgets Tarjei Vesaas-aften. Oslo. 1964. Pp. 37–40.)

DALE, JOHANNES. "Tarjei Vesaas." *Nordisk tidskrift*. Pp. 185–94. Stockholm. 1964.
HOUM, PHILIP. "Tarjei Vesaas." *Norsk litteraturhistorie*. 6. bind. Pp. 246–70. Aschehoug. Oslo. 1955.
LONGUM, LEIF. "Forlösningens mysterium: Tarjei Vesaas." *Et speil for oss selv*. Menneskesyn og virkelighetsoppfatning i norsk etterkrigsprosa. Pp. 221–30. Achehoug. Oslo. 1968.
NORDLAND, ODD. "Tid og ferd i Vesaas' symboldiktning." *Syn og segn*. Pp. 337–49. Oslo. 1957.
NAESS, HARALD. "Et forsök over Vesaas' prosastil." *Edda*. Pp. 148–75. Oslo. 1962.
For a more complete bibliography cf. Kaare Haukaas, "Ein bibliografi," in *Tarjei Vesaas*. Festskrift på 70-års dagen. Pp. 97–162. Oslo. 1967.

Index